Practice Test #1

Practice Questions

1. How can adults support adolescent development in the affective, social, and moral domains?

    a. Help teens to plan ahead for situations involving peer pressure and/or risky behaviors.

    b. Respect teen needs for privacy by not showing interest in/asking about their activities.

    c. Avoid asking about suicidal ideations, which can escalate depression common in teens.

    d. Attribute all behavior changes observed to adolescence and do not investigate further.

2. Which of the following is one way teachers can help adolescent students develop their pragmatic linguistic skills?

    a. Teach them to distinguish literal vs. figurative word meanings.

    b. Teach them the skills needed to ask others questions socially.

    c. Increase their vocabularies to increase their intellectual ability.

    d. There is no specific instruction for developing pragmatic skills.

3. When sixth-graders fail to complete assignments or act out in class, to which of the following are teachers with experience and developmental perspectives more likely to attribute such events accurately, whereas teachers without these assets are more likely to choose one of the others?

    a. ADHD

    b. Mental illnesses

    c. Behavioral problems

    d. Adjustment problems

4. Which of the following can teachers incorporate in instruction with adolescent students that they could not with younger students?

  a. Liquid conservation

  b. Deductive reasoning

  c. Reversible operations

  d. Symbolic representation

5. Of the following, which is the *most accurate* conclusion regarding cultural differences in American middle schools and high schools, particularly about school desegregation and bilingual education?

  a. Since American schools today are desegregated, the neighborhoods surrounding them must also be.

  b. Since some Latino parents feel it can overcome discrimination, bilingual education must be retained.

  c. Since school desegregation and bilingual education are both legal mandates, compromise is needed.

  d. Since some Latino parents think it ruins Latin influence and bilingual programs, desegregation is bad.

6. Which of these most describes developmental activities of *later* adolescence?

  a. Establishing realistic goals for life and pursuing them

  b. Applying cognitive skills and developing self-images

  c. Separating from parents, exploring, experimenting

  d. Developing responsibility, self-reliance, and control

7. Hands-on, experiential learning activities can further adolescent cognitive and psychosocial development. Which result of these activities is most likely to help preadolescents and younger adolescents resolve the conflict of Industry vs. Inferiority?

  a. Transitioning from concrete to abstract thought

  b. Having experiences of success in school activity

  c. Forming future action plans they find satisfying

  d. Transitioning from intuitive to logical reasoning

8. According to psychologist David Elkind, what he termed "adolescent egocentrism" includes a self-centered hypersensitivity to the perceptions of others. What did he call this?

   a. The myth of invincibility

   b. The imaginary audience

   c. The personal fable

   d. None of these

9. Researcher Robert Pianta (c. 2012) compared two approaches to changing teacher expectations. One approach was to talk to teachers, giving them information to persuade them that they held erroneous beliefs. The other approach was to give teachers intensive training in practicing different classroom behaviors. What were the results?

   a. Teachers' beliefs were changed more by the behavioral training.

   b. Teachers' beliefs were changed more by the informational talks.

   c. Teachers' beliefs were changed equally by both the approaches.

   d. Teachers' beliefs were not changed by either of the approaches.

10. Which of the following reflects expert recommendations for teacher behaviors that can change their interactions with students to address problematic student behaviors?

   a. Teachers cannot and should not try to view school through students' eyes.

   b. Teachers' own experiences with good/bad teachers/bosses are irrelevant.

   c. Teachers can list words for feelings in interactions and what evoked them.

   d. Teachers should focus on their perceptions of students but not vice versa.

11. According to experts, what is true about an effective instructional strategy that helps teaching and student learning and performance?

   a. Teachers' telling students success stories will not help them see cause and effect.

   b. Teachers should have students keep logs to help them connect efforts to results.

   c. Teachers' tangible rewards to students are more effective than symbolic rewards.

   d. Teachers should ensure equitable treatment by making student rewards uniform.

12. What is correct regarding teacher use of words and images in instruction?

  a. Visual representations are preferred since they stimulate and increase brain activity.

  b. Verbal representations are preferred for instructing students regarding relationships.

  c. Visuals are better for relationships; verbal modes are better for teaching information.

  d. Students achieve more when they are taught using both verbal and visual modalities.

13. Which of these statements accurately reflects recommended practices for giving students learning goals and feedback?

  a. Learning goals for students should be unrelated to their personal goals.

  b. Contracts are good ways to define goals and grades for reaching them.

  c. Teachers should give students general, delayed, and positive feedback.

  d. Teachers should be the only ones who lead student feedback sessions.

14. Schools can engage students in activities enabling their participation in school-based issues to promote critical thinking and ownership of learning. Which example correctly matches the student role with the associated activity?

  a. Students as planners in classroom behavior rules, new building design, choosing textbooks

  b. Students as professional development partners in showing teachers how to use technology

  c. Students as decision makers in collecting and analyzing data and team development activity

  d. Students as teachers in influencing curriculum, school policy, and school climate in governing

15. Among speech/language disorders, which category most often includes remediation via surgical procedures?

    a. Voice disorders

    b. Language disorders

    c. Articulation disorders

    d. Rate and rhythm disorders

16. Which choice correctly sequences these related behavior disorders by age groups affected, from youngest to oldest?

    a. Antisocial Personality Disorder, Oppositional Defiant Disorder, Conduct Disorder

    b. Conduct Disorder, Antisocial Personality Disorder, Oppositional Defiant Disorder

    c. Oppositional Defiant Disorder, Conduct Disorder, Antisocial Personality Disorder

    d. These behavior disorders are not related and do not affect particular age groups

17. Of the following adaptations, which most helps visually impaired students navigate school buildings and grounds and other public environments?

    a. Strobe lights

    b. Text-to-speech software

    c. Magnification and large print

    d. Orientation and mobility training

18. Tantrums, "meltdowns," interruptions, and other disruptive and/or inappropriate classroom behaviors are most common with which type(s) of behavior disorder(s)?

    a. Intellectual disabilities

    b. With any or all of these

    c. Autism spectrum disorders

    d. Attention deficit hyperactivity disorder

19. Which of the following is an example of how the variable of gender can affect student learning and performance?

    a. Visual vs. kinesthetic

    b. Cooperation vs. competition

    c. Physical vs. relational aggression

    d. Inadequate vs. adequate clothes/food

20. Whether a student has more internal or external locus of control is related to which variable influencing learning and achievement?

    a. Motivation

    b. Self-confidence

    c. Student maturity

    d. Cognitive development

21. What law(s) were models on which the Americans with Disabilities Act (ADA) was modeled?

    a. The Civil Rights Act

    b. The Rehabilitation Act

    c. The Individuals with Disabilities Education Act

    d. (a) and (b) were, but (c) under that name was not

22. Which of the following defines discriminant validity in assessment?

    a. Constructs are not combined or confounded in what a test measures.

    b. Constructs expected to be related when tested are found to be related.

    c. Constructs expected to be unrelated are tested and are found unrelated.

    d. Constructs measured by tests can be generalized to the larger population.

23. An educational researcher gives the same test to two groups of students, then delivers an instructional intervention to one group, and then gives both groups the same test again. The intervention/treatment group scores much higher this time; the control (non-

treatment) group scores essentially the same as the first time. The researcher concludes that barring other factors, the intervention was what raised one group's scores. What type of validity does this illustrate?

a. Internal validity

b. External validity

c. Ecological validity

d. Population validity

24. Which statement is most accurate in describing formal assessments?

a. They are best for formative assessment.

b. They are frequently standardized tests.

c. They are more individualized measures.

d. They are typically criterion referenced.

25. Of the following, which most correctly represents informal assessments?

a. These are supported with statistics.

b. These are best for generalized data.

c. These are best to compare students.

d. These are often performance based.

26. What is more typical of an informal assessment?

a. Assessing overall achievement

b. Improving ongoing instruction

c. Yielding more objective results

d. Being scored with percentages

27. When teachers assess student performance using continua, which is a disadvantage?

  a. More precise evaluative descriptions of student performance instead of discrete grades

  b. Greater difficulty in comparing student, class, and school scores without exact numbers

  c. Performance ranges are more realistic and accurate than exact numbers or cutoff scores

  d. Greater compatibility with individualized student assessment than standardized testing

28. Which of these do standardized ability tests measure in students?

  a. Student competence

  b. Student performance

  c. Student school grades

  d. Student mental health

29. What is correct in describing standardized achievement tests?

  a. They measure convergent and divergent thinking and domain-specific skills.

  b. They measure what students are capable of as well as what they actually do.

  c. They are formative evaluations, frequently made during ongoing instruction.

  d. They are summative evaluations, usually given at the end of the school year.

30. What do standardized achievement test results enable educators to do?

  a. They enable educators to compare students in one grade to those in other grades.

  b. They enable educators to assess student fulfillment of classroom learning criteria.

  c. They enable educators to compare an individual student's progress over the years.

  d. They enable educators to compare achievement among students but not schools.

31. Which of these do standardized ability tests and standardized aptitude tests both do?

    a. Both measure execution, not potential.

    b. Both measure potential, not execution.

    c. Both measure potential plus execution.

    d. Both measure ability and also interests.

32. What is the correct behaviorist term for strengthening a behavior by taking away something?

    a. Positive punishment

    b. Negative punishment

    c. Positive reinforcement

    d. Negative reinforcement

33. In curriculum design, what is/are included in the definition of scope?

    a. All these plus teacher expectations of student performance

    b. Breadth and depth of subject content covered in instruction

    c. Curricular coherence through longitudinal instruction in content

    d. Learning objectives reflecting national, state, and local standards

34. Which of the following represents effective curriculum design in terms of sequence?

    a. Reading before writing

    b. Writing before reading

    c. Speaking before listening

    d. Listening following writing

35. Mapping curriculum scope is a way for teachers to do which of the following?

    a. Ensure curriculum progresses in complexity and abstraction

    b. Respond to relative student interest through the curriculum

    c. Integrate state and district learning standards into curriculum

    d. Assure prerequisite knowledge and logical delivery of content

36. How do state education departments and school districts address curriculum scope and sequence?

    a. Sequencing via developmental strands

    b. (a) and (c) are common, but (d) varies

    c. Organizing scope via key learning areas

    d. States delegate them to school districts

37. What is correct about the definition of independent study as an instructional strategy?

    a. It involves only an individual student working alone.

    b. It can include individuals, partners, or small groups.

    c. It can involve paired students but not small groups.

    d. It can involve small groups but not paired students.

38. Which of the following is an example of experiential learning?

    a. Watching a video, taking notes

    b. Reading a textbook, taking notes

    c. Testing a hypothesis, taking notes

    d. Listening to a lecture, taking notes

39. Interactive learning activities can overlap with which other instructional methods?

    a. Indirect instruction activities

    b. Independent study activities

    c. Experiential learning activities

    d. With any, for certain activities

40. When should teachers write lesson plans for effective organization and implementation?

    a. After creating the plan of study, before the lesson plan calendar

    b. After a plan of study, units, timelines, and lesson plan calendar

    c. After planning instructional units, but before planning timelines

    d. After making a lesson plan calendar, before planning the units

41. Which of these is a benefit students receive from continuous student performance monitoring and charting?

    a. Students receive visual illustrations of what they learn.

    b. Students receive delayed feedback from the teachers.

    c. Students receive graphs and goals only from a teacher.

    d. Students receive practice through independent study.

42. Of the following, which do Cloze procedures involve on the part of the student?

    a. Changing closed sentences into open-ended sentences

    b. Changing open-ended sentences into closed sentences

    c. Connecting phrases or clauses into complete sentences

    d. Changing incomplete sentences to complete sentences

43. Which of these represents a caveat concerning independent instruction?

   a. Students can pursue individual interests with their own paces and styles.

   b. Students develop autonomy, initiative, self-confidence, and self-esteem.

   c. Students benefit from the high flexibility and adaptability of applications.

   d. Students must first have developed skills needed to work independently.

44. After a class unit on environmental education, one student wants to study this topic in greater depth, develop specific expertise in sustainable practices' and research various environmental jobs to consider future career paths. Which kind of learning center(s) would help accomplish all these goals?

   a. Any or all of these

   b. An enrichment center

   c. A skill development center

   d. An interest/exploratory center

45. In independent instruction, what is included in student research projects?

   a. Teachers assign research questions for students to investigate.

   b. Students develop research questions; teachers supply sources.

   c. Teachers provide guidance to students only as they require this.

   d. Students must communicate their results without any guidance.

46. What is most true about how field trips relate to student learning?

   a. Their only benefit is that students love getting out of the classroom.

   b. They have the benefits of applying classroom knowledge in real life.

   c. They confuse students when real conditions differ from classrooms.

   d. They give the benefit of interacting with nature but offer no real learning.

47. Which of the following factors is/are NOT a component of intrinsic motivation to learn?

    a. Fascination for the content

    b. Rewards and punishments

    c. Relevance to one's real life

    d. Enhancement of cognition

48. Among characteristics of intrinsic student motivation, which is an advantage?

    a. The length of time that it lasts

    b. The length of time that it takes

    c. The differentiation that it needs

    d. The length of time that it works

49. What is true about how teachers can support student development of intrinsic motivation?

    a. Teachers can interest students in content without being interested in it themselves.

    b. Teachers strongly interested in content need not show it to develop this motivation.

    c. Teachers can develop intrinsic student motivation without knowing student interests.

    d. Teachers can develop intrinsic motivation by connecting content to student interests.

50. Research-based strategies to motivate students are reflected by which teacher behavior?

    a. They are interested in students' learning but are not personally interested.

    b. They are role models, leading student motivation and passion by example.

    c. They need not believe in students' abilities as long as they indicate interest.

    d. They eschew the personalization of subject content for individual students.

51. In teacher communication strategies, what best describes the effects of some types?

    a. Utilizing media will only distract from communicating instructionally.

    b. Slide presentations demonstrate reasoning and illustrate processes.

    c. Animations and videos are best for the summarization of key points.

    d. Boards or overheads give a sense of scale, show dynamic processes.

52. Among the following instructional aids, which is best for illustrating sounds associated with physical processes?

    a. Audio

    b. Realia

    c. Artifacts

    d. Handouts

53. Multimodal presentations that offer input to multiple senses, and lessons incorporating redundant information, are beneficial to which students?

    a. English language learners (ELLs)

    b. Students who have disabilities

    c. Gifted and talented students

    d. These and all other students

54. Which of the following examples of questions that teachers can ask students access the Analysis level of Bloom's Taxonomy?

    a. Can you think of synonyms? Other examples? Can you use the word in another context?

    b. Does this fit a pattern? What effect does it have? Why do you think the author did this?

    c. Which is most effective? What are strengths and weaknesses? What are your opinions?

    d. How could you change text features, audience, etc.? Can you create your own version?

55. A teacher asks the class questions about what the main points are in a text, what happened in various text parts, and why certain events or actions transpired. Which level of Bloom's Taxonomy is the teacher addressing?

a. Understanding

b. Remembering

c. Evaluating

d. (a) and (b)

56. If a teacher wants to give students an activity to access the Synthesis level of Bloom's Taxonomy, which of these would be most relevant?

a. Having a class debate about a topic from text read

b. Analyzing author styles and adopting writing styles

c. Producing questions that are based on a text read

d. Drawing concept maps exploring text connections

57. A teacher gives the class an assignment to write criteria reflecting reader expectations for different kinds of texts. Which level of Bloom's Taxonomy does this most involve?

a. Evaluating

b. Analyzing

c. Applying

d. Creating

58. After a class has read a text, their teacher assigns students to create mind maps of a topic included in that text. Which level of Bloom's Taxonomy does this assignment access?

a. The applying level

b. The synthetic level

c. The assessing level

d. The analytical level

59. What is true about acceptable use policies (AUPs) that users must agree to before obtaining network IDs and accessing the Internet?

    a. Most public schools today have AUPs.

    b. Businesses have AUPS, unlike schools.

    c. Internet service providers have no AUPs.

    d. Only a minority of public schools have AUPs.

60. The rules of most acceptable use policies (AUPs) include which of the following?

    a. Users can post commercial messages to Usenet groups at will.

    b. AUP rules prohibit violating laws and user or network security.

    c. "Mail-bombing" websites is not prohibited by most AUP rules.

    d. People cannot prevent unwanted emails through AUP rules.

61. What is a correct statement about online search engines?

    a. Shopping, social, and information sites all have them.

    b. Social media websites do not feature search engines.

    c. Online marketplace websites have no search engines.

    d. Only sites mainly for searching like Google have them.

62. When we access and manipulate online information remotely using our computers or other digital devices, what things enable this?

    a. Hardware

    b. Databases

    c. Applications

    d. None of these

63. As an approach for managing student behavior, what is a characteristic of the "simple authority statement" from the teacher?

   a. It causes emotional distress but stops misbehavior authoritatively.

   b. It models reasonable, respectful use of authority with little upset.

   c. It expresses teacher disapproval of student behavior subjectively.

   d. It expresses teacher disapproval authoritatively, but it takes time.

64. Which of the following is most accurate about teacher redirection of students to other activities as a behavior management approach?

   a. Redirection interrupts misbehavior, but it provokes student hostility.

   b. Redirection returns behavior to on-task, but it damages self-esteem.

   c. Redirection focuses students on target behaviors, but not aversively.

   d. Redirection helps, but not as well as confronting the student directly.

65. When students display problem behaviors, which teacher response is most effective?

   a. Tell students what they should do the next time.

   b. Tell students what thing they did wrong this time.

   c. Assume younger students misbehave intentionally.

   d. Assume students with ADHD misbehave purposely.

66. What can teachers accomplish by initially responding to minor student misbehaviors with silence?

   a. They can keep themselves from responding inappropriately.

   b. They can always extinguish misbehaviors via ignoring these.

   c. They can buy time currently without informing actions later.

   d. They can think of solutions, but not allow students to do so.

67. When students behave unacceptably in classrooms, which specific teacher response most helps students to develop responsibility and self-management?

    a. Telling the students how to correct their behaviors

    b. Managing behavior when they cannot self-manage

    c. Sending the students a message to "Check yourself"

    d. Telling students to manage themselves responsibly

68. A "clock focus" strategy is useful with younger students who get restless and/or go off-task during individual classwork. What does this include?

    a. Students remain seated and watch clock minutes as the teacher designates.

    b. Students stop work and watch the clock until the teacher's signal to resume.

    c. Students stand and watch clock second-hand rotations on the teacher's cue.

    d. Students watch as many one-minute second-hand cycles as the teacher says.

69. As a classroom behavior management strategy, what does placing a student in a "visitor's chair" near the teacher accomplish if done correctly?

    a. It lets the student return to regular seating when ready to self-manage.

    b. It communicates to the student that the teacher expresses disapproval.

    c. It penalizes the student for off-task behavior by singling out the student.

    d. It deprives the student of self-regulation by giving the teacher all control.

70. Which teacher behavior is most effective for classroom behavior management that helps students learn to communicate responsibly?

    a. Tell students how to interact rather than showing them.

    b. Describe student behaviors to peers in the third person.

    c. Comment on student behaviors using the second person.

    d. Express personal feelings and needs with the first person.

71. Why do students frequently become distracted, restless, and misbehave during classroom transitions between lessons and other activities?

    a. The activities preceding the transitions are not standardized.

    b. The activities following the transitions are not standardized.

    c. The transitions between the activities are not standardized.

    d. The activities and transitions between are not standardized.

72. What is true about teachers' treating students the same way regardless of how much or little they expect from them?

    a. Doing this is easier affectively than academically.

    b. Doing this is difficult affectively and academically.

    c. Doing this is easy affectively and/or academically.

    d. Doing this is easier academically than affectively.

73. Which of these is accurate regarding teacher strategies for responding to student cultural diversity needs?

    a. To make diversity a resource, not a liability, do not give students adult responsibilities.

    b. To fill gaps in cultural capital, explicitly teach skills for studying and college preparation.

    c. To foster student participation, avoid showing personal interest in individual students.

    d. To understand student behavior in and out of class, knowing home cultures is no help.

74. How do educators support student success by encouraging active parental participation?

a. The way parents converse has no effect on their children's classroom communications.

b. Educators need not be as concerned about parent expectations as school expectations.

c. Educators can help parents pursue ESL and GED programs, which support their children.

d. Referring students' parents to community resources is outside the scope for educators.

75. Which statement is most accurate about culturally relevant instruction?

a. Making semantic webs about student experiences cannot inform lesson planning.

b. Culturally relevant curriculum aids authentic, interactive literacy and thinking skills.

c. Students' self-esteem is unaffected by curriculum on their cultures' contributions.

d. Culturally compatible norms make topics meaningful but do not affect instruction.

76. Among instructional techniques to develop oral communication skills, which one would incorporate "CROWD" and "PEER" prompts?

a. Dialogic Reading

b. Think-Pair-Share

c. Choral Response

d. Inside/Outside Circle

77. Which teaching strategy for developing written communication skills can also be used to develop spoken communication skills?

a. Written Responses, Varying Answers

b. Written Responses, Same Answers

c. None of these works for both

d. Think-Pair-Share activities

78. What is most accurate about traditional vs. cooperative organized games for preschoolers?

    a. Other than their organization, these have essentially the same effects.

    b. Cooperative games are less fun for children than traditional games are.

    c. Traditional games are better than cooperative for teaching varied skills.

    d. Preschoolers have more fun and learn more skills in cooperative games.

79. For kindergarteners, what must teachers consider in scheduling learning activities?

    a. High energy levels mean children need ongoing active movement.

    b. Extended activities are best for developing longer attention spans.

    c. Alternating movement and rest prevents exhaustion and boredom.

    d. Kindergarteners cannot work independently or cooperatively yet.

80. For younger students, which skills does play develop?

    a. Social skills but not academic skills

    b. Social and all main academic skills

    c. Literacy and math, but not others

    d. Most subjects but not technology

81. According to teachers and administrators, which is accurate about strategies for parent-teacher conferences they recommend?

    a. Parents usually resent ideas for home use from teachers.

    b. Thanking parents for attending conferences is important.

    c. Parents will not want specific suggestions on how to help.

    d. Needed improvements discussed require no follow-ups.

82. Regarding parent-teacher conferences, what reflects teacher reports of effective strategies?

    a. Blunt phrasing is the only way to get students and parents to see reality.

    b. Teachers should never include students in conferences with the parents.

    c. Some teachers let students lead conferences on report cards, portfolios.

    d. Teachers should avoid setting goals with students and parents too early.

83. What is true about teacher participation in school/district committees and activities?

    a. Teachers may only serve on committees during school days.

    b. Committee work enables problem solving for teachers only.

    c. Teachers communicate with parents, not involving students.

    d. Teacher support often determines extracurricular activities.

84. When teachers participate in committees, projects, and other school functions, which opportunities does such participation afford?

    a. More chances to pursue professional development

    b. Deciding school rules and discipline but not athletics

    c. Training in individual content subjects is not available

    d. Fundraising and crisis management but not tutoring

85. Some ways that teachers can participate in school/district projects, committees, and other activities include which of the following?

    a. Faculty, department, staff, and PTA/PTO meetings only

    b. Their participation benefits teachers more than others

    c. These do not include admissions of special populations

    d. Finding and choosing texts, and contributing to designing curricula

86. Experts report which of the following about reflective teachers relative to appraisals?

    a. Reflective teachers excel at self-evaluation but resist others' evaluations.

    b. Reflective teachers do not fear evaluations but are unlikely to self-assess.

    c. Reflective teachers want self-improvement informed by other educators.

    d. Reflective teachers are motivated to improve mainly for better appraisals.

87. How are teacher performance appraisals typically conducted?

    a. Once in every school year

    b. Once every quarter/term

    c. By teachers as colleagues

    d. By trained administrators

88. Among areas wherein appraisal systems evaluate teacher performance, what is or is not included?

    a. Effective instruction, teacher-centered or student-centered regardless

    b. Whether students participate actively and successfully in their learning

    c. Evaluation of student progress is more important than giving feedback

    d. Discipline is not evaluated like time, materials, and teaching strategies

89. What is correct about how teachers are evaluated in performance appraisal systems?

    a. Professional communication is not an appraised topic.

    b. Professional development for the teacher is included.

    c. Compliance with P&Ps for operations is not evaluated.

    d. Improvement only for identified students is assessed.

90. Rules typically established in public schools for teacher performance appraisals include which of these?

    a. Classroom observations can inform feedback given anytime afterward

    b. Classroom observations at the very ends, but not beginnings of school

    c. Classroom observations at the very beginnings, but not ends of school

    d. Classroom observations immediately preceding holidays are accepted

91. FERPA regulations allow student records disclosure without consent under which conditions?

    a. To any school officials, who need not have specific reasons

    b. To schools where students transfer so records are needed

    c. To school personnel excepting those related to financial aid

    d. To any auditing or evaluating officials with no specifications

92. According to the provisions of FERPA, when can schools furnish student records without consent?

    a. To some doing studies, if on behalf of the school.

    b. Court orders and legal subpoenas are insufficient.

    c. Safety or health emergencies still require consent.

    d. To juvenile justice system authorities in all states.

93. What is correct about FERPA regulations regarding school disclosure of student "directory" information?

    a. Schools must obtain written consent of the student's parents prior to disclosure.

    b. Schools can disclose names, addresses, and birth dates, but not phone numbers.

    c. Schools must notify parents and students of FERPA rights, but must not disclose.

    d. Schools can disclose, but with enough prior notice for requesting non-disclosure.

94. Among these professional organizations, which is/are (a) labor union(s)?

    a. The National Education Association

    b. (a) and (c) are unions, but (d) is not

    c. The American Federation of Teachers

    d. National Council of Teachers of English

95. What is true about the professional organizations available to educators today?

    a. Early childhood education has its own professional organization.

    b. Organizations exist for science teachers but not specific sciences.

    c. There is a special education group, but none for gifted education.

    d. An organization exists for teaching foreign languages but not ESL.

96. Which professional development resource most often informs teachers about the effectiveness of various instructional practices?

    a. Federal education departments

    b. Educational research studies

    c. State boards of education

    d. Local school districts

97. What is applicable regarding teacher professional development (PD) routes?

    a. Once hired, teachers usually only get PD via professional organizations.

    b. Working teachers do not have the time to attend graduate PD courses.

    c. Teachers use PD to get higher degrees/certificates in the same subject.

    d. Many teachers learn additional subjects and/or specialties through PD.

98. Among these forms of educator professional development (PD), which kind enable collaborations on presentations, workshops, etc., as well as information sharing?

    a. Mentors

    b. Study groups

    c. Learning communities

    d. Pre-service internships

99. Which statement related to teacher professional development goals and processes is most accurate?

    a. U.S. states certify/license teachers with BA/BS degrees, not expecting Master's also.

    b. Teachers earn the same licensure regardless of the PD goals of individual U.S. states.

    c. Once a teacher has an advanced graduate degree, there is no need for further goals.

    d. PD goals can include reading professional literature as well as taking specific courses.

100. Which of the following do school districts' professional development committees (PDCs) do to help educators pursue PD?

    a. PDCs work with new teachers and their mentors but never pay workshop tuition.

    b. PDCs ensure PD goals meet district guidelines and document PD for state boards.

    c. PDCs work apart from district administrators by setting only interdisciplinary goals.

    d. PDCs defer to district administrators for setting district professional teacher goals.

Answers and Explanations

1. A: As teens develop affectively, socially, and morally, adults can support their growth by helping them to plan ahead for situations involving peer pressure to engage in risky behaviors and/or involving their friends' risky behaviors. Helping them anticipate and plan is important as teens often encounter such situations for the first time. While experts advise adults to respect teen needs for privacy, they also advise adults to show interest in teenagers' activities (b). Although depression is common during adolescence, adults should ask them about any suicidal ideations (c) and other feelings, which can avert rather than precipitate tragedy. While adolescence involves many behavioral changes, adults should not attribute all of these to the life stage, but rather should investigate further (d) any marked changes in behavior causing concern.

2. B: Pragmatics is the area of linguistic development involving using language socially with other people in order to meet one's needs. One way teachers can help adolescent students develop their pragmatic linguistic skills is to teach them skills for asking questions socially. Teaching them to distinguish between literal and figurative word meanings (a) is a way for teachers to help teenage students develop their linguistic mediation skills rather than their pragmatic skills. While researchers find very high positive correlations between vocabulary and IQ test scores, vocabulary is more likely a function of intelligence than vice versa (c). Therefore, (d) is incorrect.

3. D: Although Attention Deficit Hyperactivity Disorder or ADHD (a) certainly includes inattention, short attention span, and impulsive behavior; students with mental illnesses (b) certainly can have difficulty completing assignments and/or exhibit disruptive class behavior; and assignment noncompliance and acting out in class can certainly be symptoms of behavior problems (c), teachers with more experience and developmental perspectives are more likely than those without these assets to realize such behaviors can actually be signs of adjustment problems. Many students begin middle school in sixth grade. Because schools can vary widely and because of change itself, students can have difficulty making transitions to middle school. The same applies to transitions from middle to high school.

4. B: As Piaget described, adolescents develop the ability to reason abstractly by performing mental operations. They can engage in deductive reasoning, e.g., responding to "if-then" propositions by speculating about possibilities, including hypothetical moral dilemmas as well as their personal futures. Students typically achieve what Piaget called conservation, e.g., understanding that the same amount of liquid exists despite being poured into differently shaped containers (a), by middle childhood. Being able to perform logical mental operations and reverse them (c) is also typical of middle childhood—as long as these concern concrete/physical objects, events, or examples. Symbolic representation (d), e.g., representing things using other objects, images, and words, typically develops earlier in childhood (c. 2-7 years old).

5. C: Although American schools today are legally desegregated, this clearly does not mean the neighborhoods surrounding them also are (a). Hence community racial and economic limitations strongly influence education. Some Latino parents believe it can overcome discrimination and support bilingual education, but the Bilingual Education Act rather than their support requires it (b). Some Latino parents believe desegregation impedes their objectives by attenuating Latin influences and destroying bilingual education programs, but this does not mean desegregation is bad overall (d). The most accurate conclusion is that compromise is required, particularly since both school desegregation and bilingual education are legal mandates (c).

6. A: In *early* adolescence, teens engage in developmental activities including applying their emergent cognitive skills and developing new self-images (b) based on their physiological changes. In *middle* adolescence, developmental tasks include separating from parents, exploring relationships, and experimenting with different ideas and behaviors (c), and developing responsibility, self-reliance, and greater control (d) of their learning and work opportunities and activities, as well as finding their place in society and contributing to it. In *later* adolescence, developmental activities include stabilizing their personal identities and social roles; integrating their worldviews and psychologies and making these more consistent; balancing fantasy, aspiration, and reality; shifting from self-interest to caring for and giving to others; and establishing realistic life goals and pursuing them (a).

7. B: For preadolescents and younger adolescents to resolve Erikson's psychosocial nuclear conflict of Industry vs. Inferiority (typically described as from age 7-12, but individual differences can make it earlier or later), they must experience success in school. For students to transition from Piaget's cognitive Concrete Operations to Formal Operations stage (a), teachers can start them with logical reasoning involving concrete manipulatives and then gradually progress, scaffolding as needed, to abstract reasoning without concrete objects. Forming action plans for the future that they find satisfying (c) is an activity that helps older adolescents to resolve Erikson's psychosocial conflict of Identity vs. Role Confusion. Students typically need to transition cognitively from intuitive thought to logical reasoning (d), i.e., from Piaget's Preoperational to Concrete Operations stage, during early childhood, not adolescence.

8. B: Within his definition of adolescent egocentrism, Elkind described teenagers' preoccupation with what others think of them as the imaginary audience—i.e., the unrealistic belief that everybody is paying attention to and concerned with them. Elkind described the myth of invincibility (a) as the unrealistic teenage belief that they cannot be harmed, which contributes to risky behavior. He described the personal fable (c) as the unrealistic teenage belief that nobody understands their experiences or feelings because these are unique to them. Since (b) is correct, (d) is incorrect.

9. A: Pianta found that training teachers to change their behaviors with students changed the teachers' beliefs more than communicating information to persuade teachers that their beliefs were mistaken. For example, a teacher who believed boys were naturally disruptive quashed a boy's enthusiastic, loud response, resulting in student frustration and emotional disengagement. But a teacher who did not believe boys were inherently disruptive encouraged a loudly enthusiastic boy to continue his response, only while quietly sitting instead. Teacher beliefs dictate their expectations and interpretations of student behaviors. These beliefs were changed more by behavioral training than by information (b); hence these approaches did not have equal results (c) or no results (d).

10. C: Experts recommend that teachers imagine school through their students' eyes (a) to understand them better, and reflect about their own best and worst teachers/supervisors, relevant (b) to appreciating student perspectives. Also, teachers should list five words describing their feelings while interacting with those best and worst teachers/supervisors, and specifically what those teachers/bosses did/said to evoke those feelings (c) to gain insight into students' reactions to teachers' actions/words. Teachers should not focus on how they perceive students, but instead should write how they think students perceive them (d) and would describe them, and how teacher expectations shape student perceptions.

11. B: As educator expert Robert Marzano has noted, effective instructional strategies include relating success stories to students, which reinforces their efforts in school and helps them see the causal relationship between effort and achievement. Another strategy that promotes this connection is having students keep logs and analyze them (b). Marzano advises teachers to give symbolic, not tangible, rewards to students (c) to recognize their efforts and achievements more effectively, and to personalize or individualize those rewards for each student to make them more meaningful and relevant than uniform rewards (d).

12. D: Research finds that while visual representations both stimulate and increase brain activity (a), students achieve more when taught using both verbal and visual modalities (d). For teaching about relationships between/among things, both words AND images are effective symbols (b), (c). For teaching information, physical models and movements are best (c).

13. B: One recommended way for defining student learning goals and what grades they will receive for meeting those goals is for teachers and students to write and sign contracts agreeing to goal and grade terms. Experts say student learning goals should be compatible with student personal goals, not unrelated (a). They note it is important for teachers to give students specific, timely, and corrective feedback (c). They also recommend that teachers invite students to lead feedback sessions (d).

14. A: Schools can involve students as planners in developing classroom behavior rules, new building designs, and textbook selection, and in planning coursework according to career research. When schools involve students in showing teachers how to use new technology in exchange for learning about all subjects in the curriculum, the role is students as teachers, not professional development partners (b). When schools involve students in collecting and analyzing data and contributing to team development, the role is students as professional development partners, not decision makers (c). When schools involves students in influencing curriculum, school policy, and school climate as members of student government, the role is students as decision makers, not teachers (d).

15. A: Voice disorders include, among others, impaired voice quality secondary to cleft palate, vocal nodules, or vocal polyps, all three of which can be remediated via surgical procedures to repair clefts, strip nodules, or remove polyps. Language disorders (b) are typically remediated by therapeutic, not surgical, treatment. Articulation disorders (c) are most often remediated by therapy. (Some structural defects can impair articulation and be corrected surgically, but these are rare contrasted with most articulation disorders.) Rate and rhythm disorders (d), i.e., stuttering or cluttering, are also most often remediated with therapy. (A minority of stuttering is caused by nerve damage to the brain and/or vocal cords, which typically cannot be surgically repaired.)

16. C: Oppositional Defiant Disorder (ODD) affects preschoolers as well as older children. About half of preschoolers outgrow ODD by eight years old; some develop Conduct Disorder (CD) a few years after diagnosis of ODD. CD is more severe than ODD and the most severe psychiatric disorder of childhood. Adolescents who have ODD or CD are more likely (almost 20 percent) to develop Antisocial Personality Disorder, a diagnosis only made in adults, which extends the symptoms of CD. Since these conditions are related and associated with age groups, (d) is incorrect.

17. D: Orientation and mobility (O&M) training is provided by O&M specialists and helps students with visual impairments to navigate school buildings, grounds, and other public environments more independently. In addition to training students to orient themselves and navigate in their surroundings, O&M specialists may teach cane use and work with students and their service dogs. Strobe lights (a) are adaptations to traditional sound-based fire alarms enabling deaf students to perceive alarms. Text-to-speech software (b), magnification, and large print (c) all help visually impaired students read rather than navigate environments.

18. B: Similar classroom behaviors are caused by different disorders. Students with intellectual disabilities (a) may behave inappropriately due to immaturity, lack of understanding, lack of communication skills, self-regulation deficits, and inadvertent adult reinforcement. Students with autism spectrum disorders (c), as well as those with ADHD (d) and communication disorders, may explode from frustration when their needs are not

met. ADHD students also often interrupt classes with vocalizations, speech, out-of-seat behavior, and other physical movements, etc. Some behaviors are substitutes for more acceptable communication when skills are lacking.

19. C: Gender affects student learning and performance in that boys are more likely to be aggressive physically, whereas girls are more likely to be aggressive relationally (verbally insulting others, spreading rumors, impugning reputations, etc.). Visual vs. kinesthetic (a) is an example of how different learning styles affect student learning and performance. Cooperation vs. competition (b) is an example of how different cultural backgrounds affect student learning and performance. Inadequate vs. adequate clothes/food (d) is an example of how socioeconomic status affects student learning and performance.

20. A: Locus of control is related to motivation, and particularly achievement motivation. Students with more internal locus of control attribute their successes and failures to causes within themselves, which contributes more to achievement motivation than external locus of control, wherein students attribute successes and failures to causes outside themselves. Self-confidence (b) affects motivation by facilitating attempting new tasks when high or inhibiting this when low. Student maturity (c) affects motivation in that some students have differing levels of physical, cognitive, and/or emotional-social maturity. Cognitive development (d) affects motivation in that students need differentiated instruction if their cognitive levels are higher or lower than those of classmates.

21. D: The ADA (1990) prohibits discrimination based on disability. By giving the same protections based on disabilities as those earlier given based on race, color, national origin, sex, or religion, the ADA was modeled on the Civil Rights Act (a) of 1964. By requiring federally funded schools, facilities, buildings, programs, services, and activities to give people with disabilities equal access, the ADA was also modeled on Section 504 of the Rehabilitation Act (b) of 1973. The ADA was not modeled on the IDEA (c), whose existence under that name* began in 1990 after the ADA; rather, by requiring equal access, opportunity, participation, and benefit from public facilities for persons with disabilities, it predicted the IDEA's extended emphasis and guarantee of inclusion and integration in education for students with disabilities. *(PL 94-142/EHA was an earlier incarnation with a different name: the name change to IDEA marked the extensive revisions accompanying reauthorization.)

22. C: Discriminant validity, also called divergent validity, confirms that constructs we expect to be unrelated are in fact unrelated. When constructs are not combined or confused in a test's measurement (a) as they should not be, this indicates the test has construct validity. When constructs we expect to be related are confirmed to be related (b), this indicates convergent validity. When a construct measured by a test given to a sample group can be generalized to a larger population (d), it has external validity.

23. A: When a test (or an experimental research design) shows cause and effect, it has internal validity. External validity (b) is whether or how much a test's results (or research effect) can be generalized to larger populations, other settings, measurement variables, and/or treatment variables. External validity includes ecological validity (c), i.e., how impervious a test or effect is to environmental influences, and population validity (d), i.e., how representative of the population the sample tested is and whether the sampling method used is acceptable.

24. B: Formal assessments are frequently standardized tests, which have been given to large numbers of students, data from their results mathematically calculated and summarized, and standard scores, percentiles, or stanines given. They are best for summative assessment after instruction, not formative assessment (a) during instruction. Their measurements are more generalized, not individualized (c). They are typically norm-referenced, not criterion-referenced (d).

25. D: Informal assessments are often performance-based and/or criterion-referenced tests rather than norm-referenced. They are often not supported by statistics (a) as formal assessments (like standardized tests) are. They are better for providing individualized student data than generalized data (b), which formal assessments better provide. Since they do not compare student scores to the average range of those in a normative sample, they are not used to compare students (c) as formal, norm-referenced, standardized tests are but to measure student performance against established criteria.

26. B: Informal assessments, e.g., rubrics, running records, criterion-referenced tests, performance assessments, etc., are typically used for ongoing or formative assessment to monitor student progress and help teachers improve their instruction based on assessment results. Formal assessments, e.g., standardized, norm-referenced tests, are typically used for assessing overall achievement (a); comparing students to peers; obtaining more objective results (c); and identifying in which percentiles (d) students scored, i.e., what percentage of other students' scores their scores were above (e.g., a student whose score is in the 20th percentile scored higher than 20 percent of the others). Informal assessments may show individual student scores as a percentage or number correct out of the total, one of several possible numbers on a rubric, etc., but typically do not include percentile rankings.

27. B: When teachers use performance continua for assessment, they can describe student performance evaluatively with more precision than when they assign separate grades (a), an advantage. However, for comparing assessment scores among students, classes, and/or schools, the lack of exact numbers on a continuum is a disadvantage (b). On the other hand, the performance ranges provided by continua are more realistic and accurate than assigning exact numerical scores or referring to cutoff scores (c), an advantage. Except for

comparisons (b)—in which case standardized tests are better—the superiority of continua for individualized assessment (d) is an advantage.

28. A: Standardized tests of ability, like IQ, creativity, verbal, numerical, spatial, memory, and other abilities measure student competence, i.e., their capacity rather than what they actually do, which is performance (b). Ability tests do not indicate and do not necessarily predict student school grades (c), which are also what they do rather than what they are capable of doing. Student mental health (d) is measured by some standardized tests, but not by standardized ability tests.

29. D: Standardized achievement tests are summative evaluations usually administered at the end of the school year to assess what students have learned and achieved, not formative evaluations made frequently during ongoing instruction (c). They do not measure convergent or divergent thinking, or domain-specific skills like verbal or quantitative reasoning (a) as standardized ability tests do. They measure what students actually do, not what they are capable of (b) doing, which ability tests measure.

30. C: Standardized achievement test results enable educators to compare an individual student's scores among different school years to assess the student's progress in school. They enable educators to compare individual students to grade peers, but not to students in other grades (a), since standards differ by grade. Since they are typically aligned with state standards, they can assess whether students fulfilled those standards; but being standardized, they do not enable educators to assess fulfillment of learning criteria for individual classrooms (b). They not only allow educators to compare achievement among students in the same class or grade; they also enable them to compare achievement in their school to that in other schools (d).

31. B: Both standardized ability tests (e.g., IQ tests, creativity tests, etc.) and standardized aptitude tests (e.g., preference tests, career tests, interest inventories, and tests of scholastic aptitude like the SAT) measure student potential rather than execution—i.e., what they are capable of rather than what they actually do—not vice versa (a) or both (c). While aptitude tests frequently measure abilities as well as interests, ability tests measure abilities but not interests (d).

32. D: In behaviorism, reinforcement is anything strengthening the probability of repeating a behavior. Punishment is anything weakening that probability. In behaviorism, "positive" means presenting a stimulus; "negative" means removing one. Hence positive punishment (a) is presenting a stimulus that makes a given behavior less likely. Negative punishment (b) is removing a stimulus that makes a given behavior less likely. Positive reinforcement (c) is presenting a stimulus that makes a given behavior more likely. Negative reinforcement (d) is removing a stimulus to make the behavior more likely.

33. A: In curriculum design, the scope of curriculum is defined as how much subject content the teacher covers in instruction, by both breadth and depth (b); how coherent curriculum teachers make the curriculum through teaching basic concepts in subject content over several years (c); learning objectives, clearly defined, that reflect national, state, and local standards (d); and teacher expectations of student accomplishment (a) resulting from instruction as well as how much subject content teachers must cover.

34. A: Curriculum design should sequence instruction logically to match developmental sequences. Receptive language develops before expressive language, so reading should be taught before writing (a), not vice versa (b), and listening before speaking, not vice versa (c). Also, oral language develops before written/printed language, so listening and speaking should precede reading and writing; hence listening should not follow writing (d).

35. C: Mapping curriculum *scope* is a way for teachers to integrate state and school district learning standards. A way for teachers to ensure that the curriculum progresses from simpler to more complex and from more concrete to more abstract (a) is mapping curriculum *sequence*. They can also respond to degrees of student interest in subject content (b), make sure students learn prerequisite knowledge first for certain content, and deliver content in a logical progression (e.g., from local to global environment in social studies) (d) by mapping curriculum *sequence*.

36. B: Common curriculum planning devices used by both state and district curriculum departments are to divide curriculum sequence according to designated developmental strands (a), and to organize curriculum scope according to designated key learning areas (c). While some states delegate curriculum scope and sequence to individual school districts (d) for certain subjects, they define these for other subjects.

37. B: The definition of independent study encompasses not only the individual student working alone (a), but also two students working as partners (c) or small groups of students (d) working together. In fact, teachers can even use independent study as an instructional strategy with the whole class. Regardless of the number of students, independent study is less teacher-centered/teacher-directed; the teacher functions as a facilitator and guide. Provided they have developed the required skills, students have more autonomy and choices with independent study.

38. C: Testing a hypothesis requires conducting research, e.g., doing an experiment, making field observations, or administering a survey and analyzing the results. Watching videos (a), reading textbooks (b), and listening to lectures (d)—even while taking notes—are not experiential learning activities because they do not involve hands-on learning activities in

which students participate directly. Rather than passively absorbing information, students learn by doing in experiential activities.

39. D: Interactive learning activities emphasize the sharing, exchange, and discussion of ideas, questions, activities, tasks, and learning among students. Indirect instruction (a) overlaps with interactive learning in discussion, for example. Independent study (b) overlaps with interactive learning in certain cooperative learning group exercises. Experiential learning (c) overlaps with interactive learning in role-playing activities.

40. B: Teachers should first review national and state standards, course textbooks, additional materials, and required test preparation materials; create a plan of study; plan instructional units and timelines; make a personal lesson plan calendar; and then write detailed lesson plans within each unit. They should not write lesson plans before making a calendar (a) or planning their timelines (c) for covering each unit, since these will affect the lesson plans. Writing lesson plans before planning units (d) makes no sense, as the lesson plans are components of the units.

41. A: Continuous monitoring and charting not only inform teachers of student progress with individual short-term objectives, enabling them to adjust instruction timely as needed; they also give students visual illustrations of their own learning and immediate teacher feedback, not delayed (b). Teachers can also have students make graphs of their own performance and set goals for themselves (c), enhancing student engagement in learning. However, continuous monitoring is not an activity that gives students practice through independent study (d).

42. D: Cloze procedures supply students with incomplete sentences wherein blanks are substituted for some key words; they must fill in these blanks with the correct words to make complete sentences. This teaches syntax, sequence, searching, prediction, reconstruction, linguistic relationships, and ascertaining meaning from context. Cloze procedures do not involve changing closed to open-ended (a) or open-ended to closed sentences (b), or connecting phrases or clauses into sentences (c).

43. D: One caveat concerning independent instruction is that for students to participate, they must first have developed the skills required for working independently. The ability of students to pursue individual interests in their own styles at their own paces (a); student development of autonomy, initiative, self-confidence, self-esteem (b), etc.; and the benefits to students of how flexibly and adaptably independent instruction can be applied (c) are all advantages of independent instruction rather than caveats.

44. A: Self-contained classroom learning centers supply varied, easily accessed learning materials for self-directed student learning activity. Students can independently study class topics in greater depth in enrichment centers (b), learn specific expertise related to such topics in skill development centers (c), and find out more information, like researching various careers related to these topics, in interest and/or exploratory centers (d).

45 C: Although students work more independently in research projects and other forms of independent instruction than in more teacher-directed activities, teachers still provide students with guidance, but only as needed. Teachers do not assign research questions (a); students develop these independently. Students, not teachers, also locate and access information sources (b) for research. Students write reports or papers to communicate their research results, with teacher guidance (d) if they need it.

46 B: While students love getting out of the classroom, this is not the only benefit of field trips (a): they let students apply knowledge and skills learned in the classroom to real life. Rather than confusing students (c), real-world variations inform them how reality differs from academic conditions. For example, rock samples in school geology labs typically have equal distribution, but in the real world quartz is more abundant; lab samples are often pure, but in the field rocks/minerals are more often mixed. Interaction with nature is a benefit *along with* real, hands-on learning (d).

47. B: Rewards and punishments given by teachers foster extrinsic motivation rather than intrinsic motivation. Components of intrinsic student motivation to learn include fascination with the subject matter (a); relevance of learning to real life (c); and recognition that learning enhances one's cognitive skills (d).

48 A: An advantage of intrinsic student motivation is that it has greater longevity than extrinsic student motivation via external rewards; it is also self-sustaining, unlike extrinsic motivation. The length of time it takes (b) for teacher preparation to develop it; the amount of individual differentiation it needs (c) for teachers to give different students; and the length of time it takes to work (d) for changing student behavior are all disadvantages.

49. D: To encourage student development of intrinsic motivation, teachers can interest students in learning content by having a strong interest in it themselves (a); demonstrating their own interest in the content to students (b); getting to know students and their individual interests (c); and moreover, connecting learning content to those student interests (d).

50. B: Research-based strategies found to promote student motivation include not only teacher interest in student learning, but also teacher personal interest (a) in their students' backgrounds and concerns; teacher demonstration of their own motivation and passion as role models for students (b); teacher belief in students' abilities (c) as well as interest in students; and teacher personalization of content for individual students (d).

51. D: Chalkboards, dry-erase boards, and overhead projections are useful for showing reasoning visually and teaching dynamically, as well as illustrating processes. Utilizing media need not distract (a); teachers can use media to enhance instructional communication in helping explain, clarify, and illustrate complex ideas. Slide presentations are best for organizing varied content, summarizing ideas, and emphasizing key points (b). Animations and videos are best for imparting a sense of scale and depicting dynamic processes (c).

52. A: Audio, recorded or live, is best for illustrating the sounds associated with various physical processes. Artifacts (c) and other realia (b) are both best for incorporating elements from real life into instruction. Handouts (d) are best for giving detailed visual images and printed/written verbal information to students.

53. D: All students with all characteristics—those learning English as a new language (a), those with various disabilities (b), the gifted, talented (c), and creative, and all other students, including the "average" and those without exceptionalities—receive benefits from multimodal presentations and redundant information. In general, people tend to learn more material more effectively when instruction incorporates redundancy.

54. B: Questions about whether text or other material fits any pattern, its effect(s), and why the student thinks the author used certain material, devices, or techniques access the Analysis level of Bloom's Taxonomy. Questions about synonyms, examples, and contextual word use (a) access the Application level of Bloom's Taxonomy. Questions about the material's effectiveness, strengths, and weaknesses, and student opinions of it (c), access the Evaluation level of Bloom's Taxonomy. Questions about changing text features or audiences, etc., and students' creating their own versions (d), access the Synthesis or Creation level of Bloom's Taxonomy.

55. D: By asking students what happened in text, the teacher addresses Remembering (b), the first level of Bloom's Taxonomy; by asking them why things happened and what the main points are in the text, the teacher addresses Understanding (a), the second level in Bloom's Taxonomy. These questions do not address the fifth, Evaluating (c) level, which would involve asking students what they think of the material, how effective it is, its assets and liabilities, etc.

56. B: The class activity of analyzing author styles and adopting certain writing styles is most relevant to accessing the Synthesis level of Bloom's Taxonomy, as students compare styles and use them to create something new. Debating a text topic (a), writing text-based questions (c), and drawing concept maps to explore connections in text (d) are all more relevant to the Analysis level of Bloom's Taxonomy, as students examine material and break down its components.

57. A: Writing criteria that reflect reader expectations for various types of texts most reflects the Evaluating level of Bloom's Taxonomy. An activity to reflect the Analyzing (b) level could be debating a topic from a text(s), making concept maps of connections in text, writing questions about text, etc. An activity to reflect the Applying (c) level could involve writing examples from other sources of a textual concept or feature. An activity reflecting the Creating (d) level could include studying and writing text in various genres, etc.

58. D: Creating mind maps of aspects of topics in text accesses the analytical level of Bloom's Taxonomy, requiring students to break down these aspects and examine their features. Identifying other texts, topics, or situations to which an idea in the assigned text can also refer accesses the Applying (a) level. Studying and using different writing genres, styles, text types, features, and audiences accesses the Synthesis (b) level. Using criteria for judging one's own and others' work accesses the Assessing (c) or Evaluating level.

59. A: Today, most public schools have Internet access, which means they also have AUPs in place. Many businesses (b) have AUPs. Internet service providers (ISPs) typically require customers to agree to their AUPs as a condition of supplying Internet connections (c). The majority, not the minority, of public schools (d) with Internet access have AUPs established.

60. B: Rules prohibiting using Internet access services to violate laws, or to violate user security or network security, are standard in most AUPs. So are rules prohibiting users from posting commercial messages to Usenet groups without prior permission (a). Another practice prohibited by AUP rules is "mail-bombing" websites (c), i.e., flooding them with mass emails. People can prevent unwanted emails through AUP rules (d), which prohibit sending spam or junk emails to recipients who do not want them.

61. A: Shopping websites (c) like Amazon, eBay, and Etsy, and websites belonging to companies with brick-and-mortar stores like Walmart, Home Depot, Target, Macy's, etc.; social media websites (b) like Facebook, Twitter, Pinterest, Instagram, Google+, etc.; business networking sites like LinkedIn; and information websites like Wikipedia, about.com, dictionary.com, etc., have search engines enabling users to locate specific information within their vast databases. Yahoo provides both search engine and email

service. Thus websites best known for their search engines like Google (d), Bing, etc., are not the only ones with search capability; the great majority of websites today include search engines.

62. C: Remote data access is enabled by software applications, not hardware (a). Databases (b) are electronic lists of information that can be sorted and searched by users. Since (c) is correct, (d) is incorrect.

63. B: The approach of the teacher's "simple authority statement" authoritatively stops student misbehavior with a minimum of emotional distress (a); models reasonable, respectful use of authority for students (b); and expresses teacher disapproval of student behavior as objectively as possible (c), and does so immediately (d).

64. C: Redirecting students from disruptive, inappropriate, or off-task behavior to classroom activities interrupts the misbehavior without provoking student hostility (a). Redirection returns them to on-task behavior without damaging their self-esteem (b) by calmly reminding them of assigned tasks rather than criticizing their behaviors. It helps students focus on target behaviors without communicating aversive feelings or judgments (c). Redirection is a useful alternative when it is unnecessary or unwise to confront a student directly (d).

65. A: The most effective teacher response for behavior management when students display problem behaviors is to tell them what they should do instead next time. This corrects their behavior, but prevents discouraging them by focusing on the future instead of telling them what they did wrong this time (b). Teachers should not assume that younger students (c) or those with ADHD (d) always misbehave on purpose when a lack of impulse control is often the reason. In such cases, teachers can curtail misbehavior by calmly redirecting students to learning tasks without impugning their motives.

66. A: When student misbehaviors are not significantly disruptive, teachers can keep themselves from responding inappropriately (a) as they might in reacting immediately by initially responding with silence. They cannot always extinguish misbehaviors by ignoring them (b): extinction only works when the behavior's sole function is to get attention and attention is withheld; the student eventually stops the behavior for lack of reinforcement. Silence can buy time currently, enable teachers to make mental notes to inform which actions may apply later (c), and allow students time to solve their own problems (d).

67. C: Giving students a "Check yourself" message implicitly communicates that by checking, they will realize what they must do to correct their behaviors. It is more effective for

developing responsibility and self-management to remind students to check themselves and let them realize what to do than telling them what to do (a), managing their behavior for them (b), or simply telling them to manage themselves responsibly (d) without giving them any specific means of doing so as telling them to "Check yourself" does.

68. C: In the "clock focus" strategy, the teacher prearranges a cue with students. When they get restless and/or go off-task, the teacher gives the cue and students stand and watch the second hand on the clock rotate to complete a full minute. Students decide how many rotations to watch, then sit down and resume working. They do not remain seated (a) and the teacher does not designate how many minutes to watch (a), (d). The teacher does not signal them when to resume work (b).

69. A: When done correctly, the classroom behavior management strategy of relocating a misbehaving student to a "visitor's chair" near the teacher gives the student a kind of time-out and allows the student to return to regular seating whenever s/he feels ready to self-manage more responsibly. This strategy encourages self-regulation without expressing teacher disapproval (b). It is not meant to penalize or single out the student for off-task behavior (c), but to stimulate, enable, and develop better self-regulation by the student rather than giving the teacher all the control (d).

70. D: To teach students responsible communication while managing classroom behavior, it is more effective for teachers to model honest interpersonal skills by showing them rather than telling them (a). Teachers can model honest interaction and communication by speaking directly to students rather than talking about them in the third person to peers (b), which can be humiliating. Commenting on student behaviors or making accusations in the second person (c), i.e., using "you" statements, provokes guilty and/or defensive feelings. Teachers model more responsible communication by expressing personal feelings and needs in the first person (d), i.e., using "I" statements.

71. D: The reason students frequently become distracted, restless, and misbehave during classroom transitions between lessons and other activities is that the activities preceding transitions (a), following transitions (b), and the transitions themselves between the activities (c) are not standardized. When teachers make the transitions uniform, students know what is expected of them, and the events preceding and following transitions no longer affect their behavior.

72. A: Experts find it relatively easy affectively to treat students the same way whether they have high or low expectations of them, but more challenging academically because once students are habituated to low teacher expectations, they may feel uncomfortable when teachers offer them greater challenges (although these are ultimately beneficial). Hence

equal treatment is not equally difficult in both domains (b), equally easy in both (c), or easier academically (d).

73. B: Teachers can make diversity into a resource instead of a liability by giving students adult responsibilities (a) for collaborating with educators to contribute to planning, coaching, financial and funding activities, etc., which also teaches students varied skills. Explicitly teaching skills for studying, working with teachers, and preparing for and applying to college to students whose parents never attended college helps fills gaps in cultural capital (b) for underrepresented students. Showing personal knowledge and caring about individual students fosters student participation (c). Understanding students' home cultures does help educators understand student behavior in and out of class (d).

74. C: Educators support students in succeeding academically by encouraging parents to participate actively. For example, they can help parents converse in ways that prepare their children for classroom communications (a). Engaging parents promotes mutual understanding of parent, classroom, and school expectations of teachers and students, supporting student success (b). Helping immigrant/undereducated parents pursue ESL and GED programs supports students (c) as parents in turn can better support children academically. Educators can also involve and help parents by referring them to community resources (d) with arts, sports, and science programs, homework help, etc.

75. B: When educators provide culturally relevant curriculum, students can learn more authentic, interactive language, literacy, and cognitive skills. When teachers make semantic webs about student backgrounds, this can inform lesson planning (a) by validating their experiences, which increases their engagement. Curriculum covering the contributions of diverse student cultures enhances student self-esteem (c). Setting culturally compatible norms and expectations for social learning organization and communication make instruction more effective (d), in both teaching and learning.

76. A: In Dialogic Reading, the teacher reads books with individual students/small groups, incorporating "CROWD" prompts for sentence Completion; text Recall questions; Open-ended text picture questions; Wh- picture questions; and Distancing text/pictures to student experiences. In Dialogic Reading, the teacher also uses "PEER" prompts, Prompting student text discussion; Evaluating responses; Expanding responses; and Repeating prompts on higher levels. Think-Pair-Share (b) lets students rehearse responses with partners who help with corrective feedback and elaboration to prepare for whole-class interaction. Choral response (c) involves unison student responses upon teacher cues after teacher questions, signals, and wait time. Inside/Outside Circle (d) involves students pairing up, conversing, and rotating partners.

77. D: Think-Pair-Share activities involve students' discussing assigned subjects with partners, giving each other constructive feedback, and then applying this feedback in sharing with the whole class. Teachers can use this for both spoken and written student responses. Written Responses, Varying Answers (a) involves students' checking written responses with partners, revising as needed, and reading them when teachers call on them. Written Responses, Same Answers (b) involves students' writing answers to teacher questions on boards and then holding them up upon teacher signaling. Since (d) is correct, (c) is incorrect.

78. D: In traditional games like Musical Chairs or Duck-Duck-Goose, the majority of children are left out of the fun (b) as competing is emphasized. Hence compared to traditional games, cooperative games not only are organized differently, but also have different effects (a). Cooperative games (Cooperative Musical Chairs/Islands, Cooperative Duck-Duck-Goose, Help, Robots, Cows and Ducks/Frogs and Dogs/Cats and Snakes/Chickens and Goats, etc.) teach children more varied skills, including listening, following directions, movement skills, and problem-solving skills, than traditional games (c). Thus preschoolers both have more fun and learn more skills in cooperative games (d).

79. C: Although kindergartners present as high in energy, they also fatigue quickly and thus cannot sustain ongoing active movement (a). Their short attention spans prohibit extended activities (b). Hence teachers must alternate movement activities with restful activities to prevent both exhaustion and boredom (c) in children. Kindergarteners actually thrive when assigned both independent and small-group cooperative work (d).

80. B: Play develops not only social skills (a), but also academic skills, in all of the main subject domains, including literacy, math (c), science, social studies, arts, and technology (d). For example, play develops print concepts, reading, writing, speaking, and listening in literacy; shapes, number concepts, terminology, prediction, money measurement, and time measurement in math; exploration of the physical properties of materials and of recycling in science; collaboration, developing and following rules, geographic thinking, mapping, and money use in social studies; drawing and creating things in the arts; and basic computer use and software navigation in technology.

81. B: Because parents often want their home interactions to support their children's learning, some teachers design games and other ideas for home use, which many parents welcome (a). Teachers emphasize how important it is to thank parents for attending conferences (b). Many parents attending conferences ask teachers how they can help their children with school; hence administrators encourage teachers to prepare by having specific suggestions ready (c). After reviewing a few recommended student improvements, teachers advise asking parents to follow up with them (d) in the following weeks.

82. C: Teachers report based on their experience that they can avoid antagonizing parents and students by using tactful phrasing (a) during conferences. Some teachers make a practice of including students in conferences with their parents (b). In fact, some teachers even let students lead conferences about their report cards, portfolios (c), etc. Some teachers also like to agree with students and parents to set one or two goals early (d) and then maintain communication throughout the year about progress toward these goals and future plans.

83. D: Whether or not extracurricular activities are available for students often depends on teacher support. Teachers may serve on committees both during school days and also during extracurricular events and activities (a), e.g., PTA/PTO nights and school Open Houses. Participating in committees enables problem solving for both teachers and students (b). By participating in events and committees, teachers communicate with parents and also show students their interest and support beyond academics (c).

84. A: Teacher participation in committees, projects, and other school functions affords more opportunities for teachers to pursue professional development; decide school rules and disciplinary procedures, and also supply leadership for intramural and other athletic events (b); obtain training in individual content-area subjects (c); and contribute to fundraising efforts and crisis management programs, and also provide tutoring (d).

85. D: By participating in school/district projects, committees, and other activities, teachers can contribute to curriculum design and also to text identification and adoption. They serve on a great many more committees than just faculty, department, staff, and PTA/PTO meetings (a); for example, those deciding on special population admissions (c), reviews, and dismissals. Not only teachers themselves, but others, benefit equally (b) from the individual expertise and special interest knowledge teachers contribute.

86. C: Experts report that reflective teachers have no fear of either self-evaluation (a) or evaluation by others (b), but rather want their self-improvement efforts to be informed by feedback from other experienced educators (c) and are motivated to improve mainly to serve their students best rather than to receive better appraisals (d).

87. A: Teacher performance appraisals are typically conducted annually, not quarterly or per term (b), and are not completed by other teachers (c) but rather by administrators who have been trained (d) to conduct such appraisals of teacher performance through observations of teachers and the application of established criteria.

88. B: Teacher performance appraisal systems evaluate not only whether a teacher's instruction is effective, but also whether it is student-centered (a); whether students participate actively and successfully in their learning (b); whether teachers not only evaluate student progress regularly, but also give students feedback (c) based on these progress evaluations; and not only on the time, materials, and instructional strategies that teachers use, but also their management of student discipline (d).

89. B: Professional communication is one of the areas of teacher performance typically evaluated in performance appraisal systems (a), as is the teacher's professional development (b); teacher compliance with policies and procedures, including procedures for operations (c) and other requirements; and improvement in academic performance for all students, not only identified ones (d).

90. A: Rules typically established in public schools for teacher performance appraisals include time limits for evaluators to give feedback to teachers following their observations; not making classroom observations at the very ends (b) or very beginnings (c) of school; and not making classroom observations immediately preceding holidays (d). The latter three are considered unfair since student and teacher behaviors are not typical at these times.

91. B: When students transfer schools, FERPA regulations permit the previous school to provide the new school with student records without consent, since the new school will need the student's records from past schools. FERPA also allows student records disclosure to school officials, but only if they have valid educational interests (a); to appropriate school personnel related to student financial aid (c) for purposes of determining and awarding aid; and to any auditing or evaluating officials, but only those specified (d).

92. A: FERPA provides that schools may furnish student records without prior consent to some researchers if they are conducting certain studies on behalf of the school; by court order or legal subpoena (b); to appropriate personnel in safety or health emergencies (c); and to juvenile justice system authorities, according to specific state laws (d).

93. D: By FERPA regulations, schools may disclose student "directory" information without prior consent (a). This includes names, addresses, birth dates, birthplaces, attendance dates, honors and awards, phone numbers (b), etc. FERPA requires schools to notify parents and eligible students of their FERPA rights annually, but does permit disclosure (c) of this student "directory" information—provided they give parents/eligible students enough prior notice so they can request non-disclosure (d) if they choose.

94. B: The National Education Association (a) is a labor union for educators, and the American Federation of Teachers (c) is an AFL-CIO union for teachers. The National Council of Teachers of English (d) is not a labor union, but a "professional association of educators in English studies, literacy, and language arts," according to the NCTE's self-description.

95. A: The National Association for the Education of Young Children (NAEYC) is a professional organization dedicated to young children, their families, early childhood educators, and early childhood education. Professional organizations include not only the National Science Teachers Association, but also the American Association of Physics Teachers and National Association of Biology Teachers (b); the Council for Exceptional Children, and also the National Association for Gifted Children (c); and the American Council on the Teaching of Foreign Languages as well as the Teachers of English to Speakers of Other Languages (d).

96. B: Educational research studies most often inform teachers about the effectiveness of instructional practices by evaluating them, comparing them, and synthesizing many studies of teaching practices through literature reviews, meta-analyses, compilations, etc., to identify consensus about the most effective ones. Federal education departments (a), state boards of education (c), and local school districts (d) are professional development resources that most often adopt research-based instructional practices for their teachers to apply in their classrooms, after research studies have identified these.

97. D: One teacher PD route is professional organizations' courses, workshops, and conferences, though this is not the only way (a). Although teachers must stay at school slightly longer than students, and many stay even later to complete work, school days still end earlier than other workdays; and unlike other professionals, teachers get summers off, so working teachers often take graduate courses (b), both individually and as part of advanced degree programs—not only in their original subjects (c), but often in additional subjects/specialties (d), e.g., adding science to math, ESL to English, special to regular education, etc.

98. C: Learning communities are a type of PD that enables educators not only to share information, but also to collaborate on producing presentations, workshops, etc. Mentors (a) help educators develop PD plans; observe and give feedback; share knowledge, expertise, and experience; and give support. Study groups (b) enable information exchange like learning communities, but not presentations and workshops. Pre-service internships (d) give educators close on-the-job supervision, practice, and work experience.

99. D: U.S. states typically issue teacher certification/licensure to bachelor's-degree graduates for one or two years, expecting them to gain master's degrees (or other additional certification) in the interim (a). Teachers earn more advanced licensure when

they meet goals established by their U.S. states (b). Even teachers with advanced graduate degrees must continue setting and meeting goals throughout their careers (c). In addition to adding credentials and taking courses and attending workshops, seminars, conferences, etc., reading professional literature can be a PD goal (d).

100. B: PDCs work with new teachers and their mentors to ensure teachers' PD goals meet school district guidelines, and sometimes they even pay workshop tuition (a). They also provide documentation for state licensure boards of new teachers' efforts to meet state requirements (b) by approving the teachers' PD plans (PDPs). They collaborate with school district administrators in setting both interdisciplinary (c) and subject-specific district-wide professional teacher goals (d).

Practice Test #2

Practice Questions

1. Which of the following is the most appropriate example of an assignment that a teacher can give to students in grades 10-12?

    a. Setting positive social interaction goals; distinguishing between short-term goals and long-term goals

    b. Setting long-term goals with action steps, completion dates, anticipated obstacles, contingency plans

    c. Setting short-term goals, planning action steps and time frames, evaluating levels of goal achievement

    d. Setting long-term goals; analyzing impacts of obstacles, conflicts, opportunities on goal achievement

2. Which kinds of instructional approaches best address the developmental characteristics and needs of adolescents?

    a. Providing hands-on, real-world, and authentic learning experiences

    b. Providing narrower ranges of learning materials for focus and depth

    c. Providing simpler, more concrete information, concepts, and humor

    d. Providing traditional academic content to ensure strong foundations

3. How can teachers inform educational problem solving with knowledge of human development, specifically adolescent cognitive and moral development?

    a. Assignments enabling students to view complex ethical or moral issues as black and white

    b. Assignments teaching students to view shades of gray they cannot see in complex issues

    c. Assignments considering moral dilemmas, exploring justice concepts, and solving problems

    d. Assignments addressing discrimination, racism, and sexism that the curriculum should not include

4. Which of the following educational practices would most address the adolescent characteristic which David Elkind dubbed the "personal fable"?

   a. Building student self-esteem while avoiding humiliation, harsh criticism, and sarcasm

   b. Self-expression and self-assessment opportunities in reading, role plays, and drama

   c. Furthering caring atmospheres, positive adult and peer relationships, group cohesion

   d. Explaining to students that changing allegiances are normal and friendship important

5. What is true relative to how student substance use and abuse affect development and learning?

   a. Substance use and abuse have not been found to cause, affect, or interact with any mental disorders.

   b. The use of alcohol and other drugs interferes with attention, but not motivation to learn and achieve.

   c. The damage that using substances causes is temporary and reversible, not permanent or irreversible.

   d. The brain and other major organs and systems, not fully developed, can be damaged by substances.

6. Which of the following are impacts that gang involvement can have on adolescent student learning, development, and growth?

   a. They protect members from other gangs and adult violence.

   b. They meet needs for identity, belonging, rules, and direction.

   c. They can end school, jobs, freedom, and life via criminal acts.

   d. They have all these impacts on student learning and growth.

7. Among the following statements, which most accurately reflects the roles and relationships of individuality and conformity during adolescence?

a. Although (b) is a concern in some ways, (c) and (d) often become even more important to teenagers.

b. In forming personal identities and defining social roles, asserting autonomy is teens' main concern.

c. Social pressures, teen hypersensitivity to peer perceptions, and social acceptance cause conformity.

d. Conformity to peer norms and group belonging gives teens company for facing adult responsibilities.

8. What correctly reflects a principle about helping middle and high school students with summarizing content, taking notes, studying, and using advance organizers?

a. Given time, students can often study best for tests by reviewing and revising their notes.

b. Skimming text, storytelling, and graphic images are unrelated to using advance organizers.

c. Advance organizers should be holistic and introduced after lessons but in advance of tests.

d. Questioning, clarifying, and predicting text helps students understand but not summarize.

9. Which of the following is true about teaching secondary school students how to conduct research for writing research papers?

a. In identifying sources, teaching students MLA, APA, or Turabian style will enable plagiarism.

b. In identifying sources, teaching students fair use and copyright laws can prevent plagiarism.

c. In identifying sources, teaching students about Creative Commons will guarantee plagiarism.

d. In identifying sources, teaching students to evaluate them is the sole way to stop plagiarism.

10. Regarding teacher and student roles, which statement is most accurate about instruction and learning?

a. Research studies have demonstrated that to learn, all students need teachers to give explicit instruction.

b. Research studies have found that rote memorization is most effective for learning all types of information.

c. Research studies have found when students participate actively in learning, they become lifelong learners.

d. Research studies find students become more original thinkers when taught information rather than skills.

11. Which of these best reflects the influences of home and community factors on high school teaching and learning?

a. In low-income communities, education is often superseded by economic survival needs.

b. In low-income communities, parents emphasize college more to escape a poverty cycle.

c. In low-income communities, after-school activities and learning centers are commonest.

d. In low-income communities, more students want to be the first in the family to go to college.

12. According to experts, which of these are characteristics common to all effective learning groups?

a. All students are actively involved, but teachers are not.

b. Students find group work meaningful and challenging.

c. Teachers assign students to homogeneous groups.

d. Competition is more important than cooperation.

13. When teachers assign students to learning groups, which of the following is a feature that all effective groups share?

   a. Students are assessed only as groups by teachers using one instrument.

   b. Students need social skills for groups, which are made for social reasons.

   c. Students need not understand learning objectives as the teachers must.

   d. Students believe they can achieve more learning in the group than alone.

14. Which of the following instructional strategy would most benefit students with predominantly haptic learning styles?

   a. Providing earphones with audiobooks to accompany printed texts during reading periods

   b. Providing movies that include music being studied, accompanied by richness in the video

   c. Assigning projects to interpret literature, science, etc., in variously textured constructions

   d. Assigning dance or sports movements as means of learning and demonstrating principles

15. Which of the following accurately reflects a provision of the IDEA?

   a. Separate classes/schools for students with disabilities

   b. Meeting student needs that differ among individuals

   c. Requiring IEPs for all students with/without disabilities

   d. Enacted at the same time for school and younger ages

16. Among the following laws, which specifically require schools receiving federal funds to provide students with eligible disabilities a "free, appropriate public education (FAPE)"?

   a. The ADA and Section 504

   b. The ADA and the IDEA do

   c. Section 504 and the IDEA

   d. All three of these laws do

17. Of the following, which most accurately reflects provisions of the 2010 ESEA reauthorization?

a. Rigorous school accountability for student performance; meeting diverse student needs

b. Rigorous school accountability for student performance; meeting disabled learner needs

c. Meeting the educational needs of English Language Learner (ELL) and homeless students

d. Educational needs of migrant worker, Native American, delinquent, and neglected pupils

18. Which of these was one of the provisions of the 2010 reauthorization of the ESEA?

a. Nationwide standards for English Language Proficiency (ELP)

b. Supporting migrant student transitions within each U.S. state

c. Homeless student funds allocated by Title I, not by number

d. Statewide standards for English Language Proficiency (ELP)

19. What statement is accurate regarding characteristics of today's English Language Learner (ELL) student population in the United States?

a. ELL students who speak English fluently have mastered the language.

b. ELL students are now prevalent in all U.S. states, no longer just a few.

c. ELL students are the only ones benefiting by school accommodations.

d. ELL students have higher disability incidence, proven by assessments.

20. According to research evidence-based practices, which of these is included in effective instruction of ELL students?

a. Awareness of prior ELL knowledge, characteristics

b. Placement of ELL students according to ELP levels

c. Avoiding the use of technology with ELL students

d. Selecting texts to keep from overwhelming ELLs

21. Among classroom strategies to meet all students' educational needs and ensure their participation, which of these is recommended?

a. Classroom rules should only be enforced by teachers, never students.

b. Classroom assignments should be meaningful but only in class settings.

c. Classrooms function best when students have a voice in how they run.

d. Classrooms should be organized to keep students from moving around.

22. Which of these is an advantage of essay questions in testing?

a. Requiring recall rather than recognition

b. Providing students with fewer choices

c. Enabling demonstration vs. description

d. Allowing grading to be more objective

23. Of the following, which is an advantage of multiple-choice tests over essay tests?

a. They take more time to give, answer, and grade.

b. They can cover smaller numbers of larger points.

c. They allow clearer correct and incorrect answers.

d. They do not enable elaboration or greater depth.

24. What is one advantage of portfolio assessments?

a. Not being standardized like many tests

b. Putting more pressure on the student

c. Showing longitudinal student progress

d. Excluding more student learning styles

25. Among the Wechsler tests, which would be most age-appropriate for assessing the intelligence of a normally developing nine-year-old student?

    a. WPPSI

    b. WAIS

    c. WIAT

    d. WISC

26. For a student who is nonverbal both receptively and expressively, which of the following tests would NOT be appropriate?

    a. PPVT

    b. UNIT

    c. Leiter

    d. Raven's

27. Standardized aptitude tests measure all EXCEPT which of the following?

    a. Student inclinations for certain jobs

    b. Student cognitive functioning levels

    c. Student verbal/numerical proclivity

    d. Student interest in certain activities

28. Which of these takes place first in the process of producing national or state standardized achievement tests?

    a. Publication and public marketing of the tests

    b. Administering the tests to student samples

    c. Publishing statistical analyses of test scores

    d. Proof of the validity and reliability of tests

29. What is true about statistical analyses that authors include when they publish standardized tests?

    a. They show whether and how much a test is valid and reliable.

    b. They show average scores rather than average score ranges.

    c. They do not show how many students got the average score.

    d. Distribution of scores other than the average is not included.

30. Why are many standardized tests called "norm-referenced" tests?

    a. Because they follow the "normal" format for standardized tests

    b. Because they are the norm for year-end testing in public schools

    c. Because they report average scores for student "norm" samples

    d. Because they refer to universal norms established for all testing

31. Which of these can educators accomplish by analyzing norm-referenced test results?

    a. Compare individual student performance with those in normative samples

    b. Compare average but not individual student performance to that in norms

    c. Satisfy federal but not state accountability requirements for federal funds

    d. Satisfy state but not federal accountability requirements for federal funds

32. Which of the following best reflects theoretical bases for standards-based education?

    a. Reporting annual standardized test results

    b. Giving low grades for poor initial performance

    c. Norm-referenced summative assessment scores

    d. Frequent formative criterion-referenced feedback

33. What is true regarding funding for, development of, and access to federal and state curriculum standards?

    a. The U.S. Department of Education funds and develops standards.

    b. Standards and updates are now easier to access online than in print.

    c. State education departments fund and develop these standards.

    d. Adopting the Common Core State Standards is a federal mandate.

34. Which of these is a benefit of federal and state curriculum standards and frameworks?

    a. Giving stakeholders common educational partnership language

    b. Making individual school and district systems function uniquely

    c. Varying expectations for students according to individual needs

    d. Freeing schools to focus, design, and plan their own instruction

35. When analyzing examples of student learning in Physical Education, which of the following activities are representative of the affective domain?

    a. The student reads some text about physical exercise; understands it, analyzes it, and compares it to other information sources.

    b. The student observes, imitates, practices, and perfects the specific physical skills required to engage in a specific sport s/he prefers.

    c. The student shows s/he values exercise knowledge by voluntary athletic participation and becomes accomplished in a specific sport.

    d. The student judges some information about physical exercise according to established criteria and writes a paper about the topic.

36. Which of the following correctly reflects the hierarchy of Bloom's Taxonomy in its most recent (2001) revision?

    a. Understanding information comes before remembering it.

    b. The analysis of information comes before its application.

    c. The organization is by types, not by levels of difficulty.

    d. Evaluation of information comes before its creation.

37. Which statement is most accurate about the instructional approach of using scaffolding?

    a. It ultimately moves student roles in learning from active to passive.

    b. It ultimately requires students to maintain their current knowledge.

    c. It ultimately moves learning responsibility from teacher to student.

    d. It ultimately moves teacher roles from expert to facilitator/mentor.

38. In scaffolded instruction, what is the correct sequence (first to last) of these steps?

    a. Teacher modeling, student think-alouds; student-teacher collaboration; student paired/small-group work, scaffolded as needed; independent student practice

    b. Independent student practice; student-teacher collaboration; teacher modeling, student think-alouds; student paired/small-group work, scaffolded as needed

    c. Student-teacher collaboration; student paired/small-group work, scaffolded as needed; independent student practice; teacher modeling, student think-alouds

    d. Student paired/small-group work, scaffolded as needed; teacher modeling, student think-alouds; independent student practice; student-teacher collaboration

39. Which of these instructional approaches emphasizes collective responsibility?

    a. Inquiry-guided

    b. Shared learning

    c. Learner-centered

    d. Learning community

40. Among instructional strategies that enhance communication and help students develop higher-order cognitive skills, which choice describes one correctly?

    a. Establish an atmosphere of urgency in the classroom.

    b. Require students to determine teacher expectations.

    c. Make idea transitions seamless by not declaring them.

    d. Establish organized routines; explain and follow them.

41. Of the following cognitive strategies, which most enables students to evaluate and regulate their own thinking?

    a. Metacognition

    b. Organization

    c. Elaboration

    d. Rehearsal

42. Of the following learning activities, which kind are *not* done in real life but are the *most realistic* of those not done in real life?

    a. Field trips

    b. Simulations

    c. Experiments

    d. Role-playing

43. Which statement is most correct about the following instructional strategies?

    a. Simulations using technology are no different than those without it.

    b. As instructional activities, games are entertaining but lack structure.

    c. Observations develop objectivity, detail orientation, and perception.

    d. Experiments have no effect on abstract concepts or student attitude.

44. Among interactive learning strategies, which of these is most formal and logical?

    a. Brainstorming

    b. Interviews

    c. Discussions

    d. Debates

45. Regarding brainstorming as an instructional strategy, which statement is accurate?

    a. The quantity is more important than the quality.

    b. The quality is more important than the quantity.

    c. The accuracy is more valued than the originality.

    d. Students have more ideas alone than together.

46. What is a characteristic of cooperative learning groups relative to ELL or LEP students?

    a. Their orientations are more amenable to collectivist cultures.

    b. They promote collective rather than individual responsibility.

    c. They enable asking peers what students do not ask teachers.

    d. They are better described by (a) and (c) than they are by (b).

47. Among research-based strategies to enhance student motivation, what is applicable?

    a. Students will be overwhelmed by being given too many examples.

    b. Students must be taught underlying principles directly by teachers.

    c. Students often want to know how content is relevant to their lives.

    d. Students succeed in cooperative learning groups without pressure.

48. What can teachers do in terms of assignments, goals, and assessment to motivate student learning?

    a. Design assignments that give every student the same challenge.

    b. Set, and help students set, performance goals that are realistic.

    c. Use tests scores and grades to indicate students' shortcomings.

    d. Grade tests on a curve to enable all students to get high grades.

49. Among the following, which is a research-based teacher practice that stimulates student motivation to learn?

    a. Providing criticism that focuses on student errors

    b. Criticizing specific performances, not performers

    c. Categorizing students into leaders and followers

    d. Controlling all learning, evaluation, performance

50. According to a model of intrinsic motivation for academic achievement, what do students do first relative to engaging in learning activities?

    a. They first engage in activities that they find interesting.

    b. They first evaluate activities on the basis of two criteria.

    c. They first disengage in activities not interesting to them.

    d. They first engage in activities with extrinsic motivations.

51. What most accurately cites goals teachers accomplish by using effective active listening strategies?

    a. They help students establish emotional connections with school rather than motivation.

    b. They demonstrate that teachers care about students without developing relationships.

    c. They show teacher attention to student concerns, while achieving multiple other goals.

    d. They are more important to help students feel understood than as models for listening.

52. Which of these most reflects a technique used in active listening?

    a. Giving nonverbal as well as verbal signals

    b. Not distracting a speaker with questions

    c. Repeating what a speaker says verbatim

    d. Not interpreting what the speaker says

53. When an active listener offers interpretations of what a speaker says and the speaker then refines these, what does this process accomplish for the speaker?

    a. The speaker is less likely to feel heard by the other.

    b. The speaker gains insight into his/her own feelings.

    c. The speaker is unlikely to have emotional catharsis.

    d. The speaker develops focusing and inference skills.

54. What is correct about the effects of nonverbal communication on listening?

    a. Listeners communicate receptivity by maintaining open postures.

    b. Listeners communicate interest in speakers via crossed arms/legs.

    c. Listeners use gestures consciously but should do so unconsciously.

    d. Listeners convey the same things across cultures with eye contact.

55. Among the following indicators of nonverbal communication, which expresses the same emotions universally across individuals, relationships, situations, and cultures?

    a. Eye contact

    b. Social space

    c. Personal space

    d. Facial expression

56. What is true about what we do via eye contact when communicating with others?

    a. We convey interest rather than hostility

    b. We express anger more than affection

    c. We gauge how others are responding

    d. We use other ways to maintain flow

57. How does nonverbal communication inform verbal communication?

  a. It can reinforce rather than contradict verbal messages.

  b. It can complement but not substitute for verbal signals.

  c. It can repeat, complement, or add to verbal messaging.

  d. It can emphasize rather than replace verbal messaging.

58. A minister with a good sense of humor relates one of his notes to himself for delivering a sermon as, "Weak point—pound pulpit." Which relationship of nonverbal to verbal communication does this illustrate?

  a. Verbal communication reinforces nonverbal communication.

  b. Nonverbal communication reinforces verbal communication.

  c. Verbal communication is replaced with a nonverbal message.

  d. Nonverbal communication repeats the verbal content stated.

59. To evaluate information found online, what is the *first* step a user should take?

  a. Read reviews of it by other users

  b. Consider the author's credentials

  c. Make a critical analysis of content

  d. Ascertain the proposed audience

60. Which of the following is something to consider during an initial appraisal of online information, such as a journal published electronically?

  a. Whether a journal published online is a secondary source

  b. Whether a journal published online is too simple a source

  c. Whether a journal published online is too technical to use

  d. Whether a journal published online is scholarly or popular

61. Following an initial appraisal of a website as an information source, which of these should the user do as part of a more thorough content analysis?

    a. Determine who published the information and if they are reputable

    b. Determine whether the information given on the site is still current

    c. Determine whether the information is fact, opinion, or propaganda

    d. Determine some background information about the website author

62. Regarding some benefits of technology to students, what is most correct?

    a. Notes are not completed enough to copy and paste into a composition.

    b. Students need not know spelling/grammar with spell/grammar checks.

    c. Moving text around easily helps students learn to organize their writing.

    d. Students must extensively organize and edit data as spreadsheet input.

63. How can teachers best design a uniform transition between activities to keep students on-task?

    a. By creating one single mini-routine

    b. By chaining several mini-routines

    c. By creating various mini-routines

    d. By a big routine of mini-routines

64. What is the most accurate description of standard transitions that teachers design to bridge smoothly between classroom activities?

    a. If the teacher simply models the transition process, the students will learn it.

    b. The teacher need not model, but must explicitly teach students the process.

    c. Teachers need not model or teach, but must practice transitions consistently.

    d. Teachers must model, teach, and practice uniform transitions with students.

65. When a teacher has designed a regular transition between class activities for students to follow, the first step in the transition should be to signal for the class to pay attention. After this, what is the next step the teacher should take?

    a. Tell students which lesson they are about to begin.

    b. Observe student activities and following directions.

    c. Ask students if anybody does not know what to do.

    d. Give students detailed directions and advance cues.

66. If a teacher has designed and implemented a uniform transition between activities in the classroom and any student(s) do(es) not follow it, what is the best recourse?

    a. Interrupt the transitional activity to correct them.

    b. Administer a standardized student punishment.

    c. Have the student(s) repeat the entire sequence.

    d. Separate them from class to avoid interference.

67. Researchers have found the most effective teachers devote the first few weeks of school to which of these?

    a. Teaching an overview of the year's content

    b. Teaching classroom routines and procedures

    c. Teaching the first set of lessons in the first unit

    d. Teaching students the social skills they will need

68. What is the best way for a teacher to instruct students in classroom procedures?

    a. Teach one or two key procedures a day for several days.

    b. Teach all procedures together and complete in one day.

    c. Hand out and go over procedures on the first day alone.

    d. Avoid explaining reasons for and modeling procedures.

69. What is the purpose of functional behavior analysis?

    a. To teach students behaviors that are functional

    b. To analyze whether a behavior is functional or not

    c. To make the analysis of any behaviors functional

    d. To ascertain the functions of any given behavior

70. Which of the following are NOT foremost learning benefits of behavior contracts?

    a. Verbal obligations and responsibility

    b. Observational and vicarious learning

    c. Self-control and self-monitoring skills

    d. Skills in negotiating and compromising

71. To inform developmentally appropriate behavioral expectations of students, what should teachers consider about K-12 student cognitive characteristics in general?

    a. They are adept at anticipating consequences of behaviors in advance.

    b. They can understand causal relationships, even if separated far apart.

    c. They are present oriented, finding that future consequences seem unreal.

    d. They have mastered time concepts and developed skills for planning.

72. What accurately reflects a principle of communicating teacher expectations to students?

    a. "Do as I say, not as I do" is a principle that applies in this instance.

    b. Starting out with achievement contracts is one effective method.

    c. Teachers should reinforce expectations periodically for students.

    d. Teachers should tell parents their expectations for students only.

73. Which of the following most correctly describes an effective teacher method for informing students of their expectations?

    a. Some students are motivated by knowing teachers as real people.

    b. Becoming the students' friend will motivate them to work harder.

    c. Having students suggest class improvements is counterproductive.

    d. Making poor grades final and moving on fosters mastery learning.

74. Regarding teaching, learning, and achievement, what has research found about student-teacher interactions and relationships?

    a. Teacher-student relationships influence student behavior but not academic achievement.

    b. Teacher-student interaction, communication, and feedback make learning more effective.

    c. Students' respect for peers promotes active learning; their respect for teachers inhibits it.

    d. The literature omits research into teacher-student relationships relative to achievement.

75. What results do student-student interaction and communication typically include?

    a. Most, but not all, students have a voice in small-group discussions.

    b. Students are no more likely to share the responsibility for learning.

    c. Students benefit from interactions without affecting class direction.

    d. Students receive exposure to, and can discuss, diverse viewpoints.

76. What have many research studies found regarding teacher enthusiasm?

    a. Teacher enthusiasm is found to have no effect on student learning.

    b. Teacher enthusiasm is found to enhance student learning by itself.

    c. Teacher enthusiasm with constructive feedback enhances learning.

    d. Teacher enthusiasm improves presentation, not positive feedback.

77. Which of these is most accurate about nonverbal teacher behaviors relative to their reflecting teacher enthusiasm and other effects?

   a. Effective teachers use their eyes to show excitement, not listen to students.

   b. Effective teachers use gestures to communicate enthusiasm, not emotions.

   c. Effective teachers use nonverbal behaviors to reinforce verbal expressions.

   d. Effective teachers move around the classroom only for monitoring reasons.

78. "Five I's" are components of innovation curriculum (Hiam, 2011): Imagination, Inquiry, Invention, Implementation, and Initiative. Which one is the foundation enabling the others?

   a. Inquiry

   b. Initiative

   c. Invention

   d. Imagination

79. Which of the following instructional practices most promotes the innovation curriculum component of Imagination?

   a. Writing across the curriculum

   b. Most questioning by students

   c. Giving students more practice

   d. Enabling student self-efficacy

80. Augmentative Alternative Communication (AAC) devices and systems can be low-technology, mid-technology, or high-technology. Which of these assistive communication devices/systems are considered the most high-technology?

   a. Dry-erase boards

   b. Overhead projectors

   c. Text-to-speech software

   d. Simple and complex VOCAs

81. How can mentors assist teachers in their instructional activities?

    a. They cannot help them address gaps in student content knowledge.

    b. They know no more specialized vocabulary than newer teachers do.

    c. They can help them decide how to allocate content area emphases.

    d. They are unlikely to offer them resources for accessing information.

82. In which of these ways can mentors use their experience to help newer teachers?

    a. Mentors can help in planning units, but teachers must address performance standards.

    b. Mentors can help in developing higher cognitive skills more than lifelong learning skills.

    c. Mentors can help in planning lessons, but only teachers can connect these coherently.

    d. Mentors can help in planning for extending and applying text and teacher information.

83. The greater experience and expertise of teacher mentors can support newer teachers in which of the following aspects?

    a. Understanding appropriate amounts of material to cover in each lesson

    b. Understanding students' greater need for reviews than clear directions

    c. Understanding that application of learning supersedes prior knowledge

    d. Understanding that task difficulty levels should be randomly alternated

84. What does research show about teacher collaboration in K-12 public schools?

    a. Teacher collaboration has no relationship with retaining new teachers.

    b. Teacher collaboration correlates positively with student achievement.

    c. Teacher collaboration is unrelated to personal satisfaction in teachers.

    d. Teacher collaboration is funded and utilized in the majority of schools.

85. Which of the following do experts recommend to foster teacher collaboration?

   a. Cultivating senses of individual responsibility in all faculty members

   b. Recruiting experienced teachers for induction and mentoring only

   c. Recruiting experienced teachers in professional development only

   d. School leaders' earmarking resources for supporting collaboration

86. According to case study research, how do teachers most commonly collaborate?

   a. Case study research finds that teachers commonly collaborate by doing all these

   b. Meeting to review student work and standards, and improve instruction accordingly

   c. Forming teams to self-plan professional development and vertically align lessons

   d. Regular lead teacher/coach support, data access, and sharing their planning time

87. According to U.S. Secretary of Education Arne Duncan, what will shape public education for future decades?

   a. Attracting the greatest quantity, rather than quality, to the teaching profession

   b. Retaining the most talented teachers as opposed to attracting more new talent

   c. Strengthening the teaching profession with only minimal changes to the culture

   d. Requiring massive cultural change yet attaining extraordinary long-term impacts

88. Which of these is most correct about the TEACH.org project for educational reform?

   a. It is a public project of the federal government.

   b. It is a private project of the Microsoft Corporation.

   c. It is a public-private partnership of ED and Microsoft.

   d. It is without relationship to the Project RESPECT of ED.

89. What is true about partnerships of schools with families and communities?

 a. Schools can use family and community strengths and needs to develop partnerships.

 b. Effective family and community partnerships improve learning for certain students.

 c. Connections between curriculum and real-world skills are shown via other methods.

 d. Partnerships of school, community, and families benefit some, but not all, partners.

90. Regarding school involvement with their communities, which of the following do community needs assessments help school action teams to develop?

 a. Approaches for community outreach only

 b. Involvement goals leading to full policies

 c. Full policies for involvement immediately

 d. Involvement program goals, not policies

91. What is true about professional development (PD) goals that teachers set and how PD committees (PDCs) help them with these?

 a. PDCs offer training to all teachers, focusing on their school districts' goals.

 b. Teacher, mentor, and PDC goals must only meet school district standards.

 c. PDCs offer training but do not work directly with individual new teachers.

 d. The SMART requirements for writing objectives do not apply for PD goals.

92. Resources like the International Society for Technology in Education (ISTE) help educators do which of these?

 a. Develop technology-based professional development programs only

 b. Integrate technology into instruction as well as develop PD programs

 c. Integrate technology into teaching rather than develop PD programs

 d. Teach educators how to use technology but not set/teach standards

93. In-depth professional development (PD) knowledge and standards for educational technology use are taught by the International Society for Technology in Education (ISTE). What would you expect this training to include?

    a. Conditions essential for implementing standards at all these levels

    b. Conditions essential for implementing standards in the classrooms

    c. Conditions essential for implementing standards at the school level

    d. Conditions essential for implementing standards for whole districts

94. The International Society for Technology in Education (ISTE), as an example of a resource for integrating technology into teaching and professional development, includes among other offerings Digital Citizenship and Technology Leadership Institutes, a Standards Readiness Workshop, and an Essential Conditions Readiness Survey to which of these personnel?

    a. Any and all public school personnel

    b. Only teachers and similar educators

    c. School principals and administrators

    d. Faculty and administrative workers

95. Which statement is most accurate about reflection relative to effective teaching?

    a. Hindsight is 20/20, so there is no point in reflecting on one's past practices.

    b. When reflecting, teachers as just as subjective as they are in the moment.

    c. Reflection enables analyzing and improving interactions but not instruction.

    d. Reflection enables improving interactions and instruction based on analysis.

96. How can teachers self-assess their classroom effectiveness using reflection?

    a. Wait long enough in the year to establish routines before taking baselines.

    b. Make video recordings of all classes to be objective rather than journaling.

    c. Select a few students with average class achievement to track relationship.

    d. Write honestly in journals and reread entries regularly to change behavior.

97. Among the following reflective methods, which is most suited to helping teachers systematically evaluate their instructional practices, address their teaching weaknesses, and expand their teaching strengths?

   a. Peer assessment or "critical friend"

   b. Making systematic incident analysis

   c. Pre-designed self-assessment tools

   d. Collecting and reviewing portfolios

98. According to cognitive research, which of these is better for reading comprehension than for complex concept comprehension?

   a. Summarizing

   b. Contrasting

   c. Comparing

   d. Classifying

99. Which higher-order cognitive skills are developed by effective summary and note taking?

   a. Analysis, in-depth study, synthesis, and reading comprehension

   b. Analysis of learning material but not in-depth, and not synthesis

   c. Synthesis of materials but not analysis or reading comprehension

   d. Summarizing, contrasting, comparing, and classifying, not analysis

100. Research into educational achievement motivation has found which of these?

   a. Students respond better to concrete rewards than they do to abstract recognition.

   b. Rewards are most effective when they are not contingent on meeting standards.

   c. Eight-year-olds use learning strategies different from those used by 12-year-olds and adults.

   d. Negative and positive feedback are both equally effective with eight-year-old students.

Answers and Explanations

1. B: Setting goals for positive social interactions and distinguishing between short-term and long-term goals (a) are appropriate assignments for students in middle school or grades 6-8. Setting short-term goals (e.g., for a hobby, sport, learning a musical instrument, or other activity of interest), planning action steps and time frames for these goals, and evaluating their levels of goal achievement (c) are appropriate assignments for students in grades 8-10. Planning long-term goals, identifying who helped them achieve a goal, and how, and analyzing the impacts of obstacles, unexpected opportunities, scheduling conflicts, and other positive and negative factors on goal achievement (d) are assignments appropriate for students in grades 9-11. Setting long-term goals that include action steps, completion dates, anticipated obstacles, and contingency plans (b) are appropriate assignments for students in grades 10-12. Analyzing present health behavioral impacts on long-term goals, evaluating the feasibility of summer job goals, self-evaluating goal achievement, creating behavioral contracts supporting coping strategies, and journaling goal progress are also good assignments for grades 10-12.

2. A: Adolescents much prefer active, interactive, hands-on, real-world, and authentic learning experiences over passive, teacher-centered lessons that describe subjects without letting students experience them directly and learn by doing. Because of the wide variety of cognitive levels and interests among adolescents, teachers need to provide wide varieties of materials, not narrower ranges (b). As adolescents develop abstract thought, teachers need to provide the more complex, abstract information, concepts, ideas, and sophisticated humor they can now appreciate rather than simpler, more concrete material (c). Teens, particularly young teens, are not as interested in traditional academic content (d) as in real-life and authentic learning. They can learn the same content through more direct hands-on experiences, which make it more real and valuable to them, enabling better retention, generalization, transfer, and application to life.

3. C: Adolescents develop the ability to see complex ethical and moral issues not in black and white (a) as younger students do, but in more realistic shades of gray. It is not that they cannot see these (b); rather, adolescents are aware of these nuances but not yet ready to confront them, raising their risk for making faulty ethical or moral decisions. Teachers can use their knowledge of these developmental characteristics to inform their instruction by providing assignments requiring adolescent students to consider moral dilemmas and responses thereto; explore justice, equity, and fairness concepts; solve problems (c); and develop their own values and set their own behavioral standards. While teachers' assignments should address discrimination, racism, sexism, and similar issues, school curriculum should also do so (d).

4. B: What Elkind named the "personal fable" is the adolescent delusion that one's problems are completely unique and nobody else has experienced and can understand or relate to them. Providing opportunities for self-expression and self-assessment through reading, role-play, and drama can help teenage students realize that their problems are not unique

but are in fact common, even universal. Building student self-esteem and avoiding humiliating, harshly criticizing, or sarcastically speaking to/about them (a) would address the adolescent characteristics of low and fragile self-esteem, exaggerated self-consciousness, and hypersensitivity to criticism. Promoting caring atmospheres, positive adult and peer relationships, and group cohesion (c), and explaining to students that changing allegiances are normal and friendship is important (d), would both help to support adolescent identity formation.

5. D: In adolescence, the brain, nervous system, heart, lungs, liver, kidneys, and other major organs and systems are still not fully developed yet, and are thus more vulnerable to damage from using alcohol, drugs, and other substances. For example, myelination, i.e., the development of coating sheaths that facilitate neural transmission and protect brain and nerve cells, which normally continues into adulthood, can be disrupted by substance abuse. Research confirms that using substances can precipitate and/or exacerbate mental disorders (a) including anxiety, depression, paranoia, bipolar disorder, schizophrenia, and others. Using alcohol and other drugs interferes not only with attention, but also with memory and motivation to learn and achieve (b). Using substances can cause temporary, reversible, permanent, and irreversible damage (c).

6. D: Although most adults know gangs encourage and/or peer-pressure adolescent members into criminal acts that can end their educations, jobs, freedom, and ultimately lives (c), not everyone realizes gangs also confer certain benefits, e.g., protecting teens against violence from other gangs and adult criminals (a), and meeting needs for behavioral direction, personal identity, group belonging, and rules (b). Adversarial relationships are more secure than complex, equivocal, uncomfortable realities; concrete foes are more beatable than larger, more abstract foes like crime, no opportunities, discrimination, illiteracy, and poverty. Hence gang involvement both negatively and positively affects adolescent development and learning.

7. A: Although in terms of separating from parents, forming their personal identities, and defining their social roles, asserting their autonomy is important to adolescents (b), it is typically not their only or most important concern. Hypersensitivity to peers' perceptions and concern with social acceptance are hallmarks of adolescence, motivating teens to conform to group norms (c). Conforming and belonging to groups not only relieves their hypersensitivity to criticism and exaggerated self-consciousness, but also helps teens feel they are not alone in facing coming adult responsibilities (d), which they may feel threatened by in defining their individuality.

8. A: When middle and high school students learn to take good notes on class lectures and lessons, reviewing and revising those notes are often the best ways for them to study for tests. Skimming text, storytelling, and using graphic images are ways of varying style in advance organizers (b), which should be analytical and introduced before lessons (c).

Having students question, clarify, and make predictions about texts helps them not only understand, but also summarize (d) better.

9. B: When helping students conduct research for writing papers, it will not enable plagiarism to teach them MLA, APA, Turabian, or other official styles (a) of citing and listing references; rather, it will prevent it. So will teaching students the regulations for fair use and copyright laws (b). Teaching students about Creative Commons licensing will not guarantee plagiarism (c) but will help students avoid it when they use Creative Commons sources. Teaching students how to evaluate sources is not the only way of preventing plagiarism (d), but a way of helping students develop critical thinking skills they will use for the rest of their lives.

10. C: Research studies find that students become lifelong learners when teachers allow and require them to participate actively in learning. Some students do need explicit instruction, but not all do (a). Research finds that rote memorization is effective for learning only factual information, not all types (b). Teaching learning and thinking skills to students produces more original thinkers than only teaching them information (d).

11. A: Regardless of student and parental interest in education, just surviving economically often supersedes it. Parents in high-income communities more often have attended college and thus expect their children in high school to attend college as well (b). Educational resources and supports like after-school activities, learning centers, tutoring centers, and stores selling educational products are commoner in high-income than low-income communities (c). Although some students in less educated families and low-income neighborhoods are motivated to be the first in their families to attend college, those who do are in the minority rather than the majority (d).

12. B: In all effective learning groups, teachers give group assignments that students find meaningful and that challenge them. Teachers are always actively involved (a) in group learning processes as coaches, guides, questioners, evaluators, and resources. Teachers assign students to heterogeneous groups (c). Cooperation is always more important than competition (d) in cooperative learning groups and their work.

13. D: One feature shared by all effective learning groups is that students believe they can achieve more by learning in the group with classmates than they could by learning on their own. In all effective learning groups, teachers are able to assess students both individually and as groups, and by using multiple, varied assessment instruments (a). Students do need social skills for interacting in groups; however, groups are not made primarily for social reasons (b). Just as teachers must understand group learning objectives, they must also ensure that students also clearly understand them (c).

14. C: Haptic learning styles favor the sense of touch and respond to tactile stimuli. Choice (a) would most benefit students with predominantly auditory learning styles that favor the sense of hearing. Choice (b) would most benefit students with predominantly visual learning styles that favor the sense of sight. Choice (d) would most benefit students with predominantly kinesthetic learning styles that favor physical movement.

15. B: The Individuals with Disabilities Education Act (IDEA) provides a guarantee of the right to a free, appropriate public education (FAPE) in the least restrictive environment (LRE) that can meet their educational needs for students with disabilities. The purposes of the LRE clause are to *prevent* separate/segregated classes/schools for these students (a), and to meet individually differing student needs (b). The IDEA requires IEPs for all students with disabilities, but not for students without disabilities (c). It was enacted initially for school ages (IDEA Part B); another section (IDEA Part C) was added later for early childhood ages (d).

16. C: Section 504 of the Rehabilitation Act of 1973 and the Individuals with Disabilities Education Act both specify a FAPE as a requirement for schools receiving federal funding to provide for students with disabilities. The Americans with Disabilities Act (ADA) (a), (b), (d) prohibits discrimination based on disabilities in access to public buildings, facilities, programs, services, and activities, including public schools. It does not specifically require providing a FAPE.

17. A: The 2010 reauthorization of the Elementary and Secondary Education Act (ESEA, aka No Child Left Behind) provides for rigorous school accountability for student performance and also for meeting the needs of diverse students. These include students with disabilities (b); ELL students; homeless students (c); migrant workers' children; Native American students; delinquent students; and neglected students (d). Only (a) summarizes all these; all the other choices omit a number of these provisions.

18. D: One of the provisions of the ESEA's 2010 reauthorization was for each state to implement statewide, *not* nationwide (a), standards by grade level for ELP. Another provision was to support the *interstate*, not within-state (b), transitions of migrant students into local schools and communities. An additional provision was to allocate funds for homeless students by number of students, *not* by Title I shares (c) as was previously provided.

19. B: Whereas ELL students were prevalent in only a few U.S. states in the past, today they are in every state. Teachers should not assume speaking fluent English indicates mastery of the language (a): basic English spoken in everyday social interactions differs markedly from

academic English; proficiency can only be assessed through systematic academic assessments. Accommodations implemented by schools for ELL students benefit not only those students, but also native English-speaking students (c). ELL students do NOT have more disabilities (d): research has proven that assessment instruments failing to separate ELL status from disability lead to misdiagnosing ELLs as disabled.

20. A: Knowing what prior knowledge and experiences ELL students have, as well as their individual learning characteristics (e.g., strengths, weaknesses, styles, preferences, etc., in their native languages) enable teachers to make their instruction effective. Placement of ELL students should be according to their academic achievement, NOT their ELP (English Language Proficiency) levels (b). Teachers should not avoid using technology (c), which helps ELLs be motivated to learn, develop English-language writing and editing skills, communicate in English print as well as speech, and collaborate on class blogs and websites. Another practice found effective in instructing ELLs is to give them choices of texts (d).

21. C: Classrooms are found to function best when students have a voice in how they run rather than having school districts, administrators, and teachers dictate this. Teachers should also assign students to enforce classroom rules (a). Teachers should give assignments that are not only meaningful to students, but are also completed in real-life settings rather than only in class (b). They should also organize their classrooms to enable students to move around (d), access information and technology easily, and visit centers or stations for long-term learning activities.

22. A: Essay questions require students to recall, i.e., retrieve information from memory without seeing it, rather than simply recognize correct and incorrect information provided as in multiple-choice tests. Essay questions afford students more choices, not fewer (b), as they can choose subtopics, points to make, examples to give, differential emphasis, various organizational methods, the option to use argumentation, etc., whereas multiple-choice questions only offer choices of several answers. Essay questions require description, not demonstration (c); performance measures enable demonstration, which benefits students who cannot write as well as they can do things. Grading essay questions is more subjective (d) than grading multiple-choice or other objective questions.

23. C: Multiple-choice questions have clearer correct and incorrect answers, whereas essay questions allow every individual student to answer differently, requiring more judgment of teachers in grading them. Multiple-choice tests take much less time to administer, answer, and score (a)—and may even be scored electronically instead of by teachers—than essay tests. They can cover larger numbers of smaller points, not vice versa (b), compared to essays. The fact that they do not enable students to elaborate or go into greater depth (d) to show more of their knowledge is a disadvantage, not an advantage, of multiple-choice tests.

24. C: Portfolios accumulate student products over longer time periods like semesters or school years, giving the advantage of showing their longitudinal progress better than a single test or paper. The fact that portfolio assessments are not standardized like many formal tests are (a) is not an advantage but a disadvantage, as the results are less objective and uniform and more subjective and variable. Portfolios put less pressure on students (b) by letting them work more gradually than on more time-limited tests. Portfolios include more student learning styles (d) and can demonstrate nonverbal and other types of skills that tests or papers cannot.

25. D: The Wechsler Intelligence Scales for Children (WISC) is for assessing IQ in students aged from 6 years to 16 years 11 months. The Wechsler Preschool and Primary Scales of Intelligence or WPPSI (a) is for assessing IQ in children aged from 2 years 6 months to 7 years 7 months. The Wechsler Adult Intelligence Scales or WAIS (b) is for examinees aged 16 years to 90 years 11 months. Wechsler Individual Achievement Test or WIAT (c) is not for assessing intelligence; it is an achievement test.

26. A: The Universal Nonverbal Intelligence Test or UNIT (b), Leiter (c) International Performance Scale, and Raven's (d) Progressive Matrices are all intelligence tests designed to be completely nonverbal. The Peabody Picture Vocabulary Test or PPVT (a) does not require students to speak, write, or sign; they can simply point to pictures (physically disabled students can use directional eye gaze or adaptive equipment), so it does not require expressive language; however, it does require receptive language to understand the examiner's verbal prompts. Hence it would not be appropriate for a student who is both receptively and expressively nonverbal.

27. B: Standardized aptitude tests measure student inclinations for specific job areas; for example, they may identify student ability and interest in teaching, mechanical work, or writing; composing, producing, and/or performing music; dancing and/or choreography; drawing, painting, and/or sculpture; mathematical computation; writing computer code, etc. Some aptitude tests measure student ability and interest for types of activities (d) rather than specific jobs/job areas, e.g., working outdoors, working with books, building things, fixing things, communicating with others, etc. Some test student proclivity for broader domains, like verbal or numerical thinking and activities (c). Aptitude tests can measure all these, EXCEPT student levels of cognitive functioning (b), which IQ/ability tests measure.

28. B: After designing a standardized test like a national or state achievement test, the authors must first administer it to groups of students they have selected as representative samples of the larger target population. The next step is conducting and publishing statistical analyses of the student samples' test scores (c). Statistical analysis proves the test's validity and reliability (d) and the numerical degree of each. Following these, the authors can publish and market their test (a).

29. A: Statistical analyses of standardized tests indicate whether the test has been found statistically valid (i.e., whether it tests the construct it is supposed to test), reliable (i.e., whether the test can be replicated with consistent results across administrations, raters, and/or within itself), and to what degree numerically. They may identify the average score received in student sample groups, *or* the average score range (b) depending on the authors and test. They *do* indicate the percentage of students receiving the average score or score range (c). They also *do* include how all other scores are distributed (d) in addition to the average score/range.

30. C: Standardized tests that are called "norm-referenced" are tests that have first been administered to samples of students found representative of a test's intended student population, and their average scores determined (as well as the distribution of all other scores beyond the average score/range) so educators administering them thereafter can compare their students' scores to these averages, which are used as norms—i.e., typical scores for students in that population. The term "norm-referenced" does not refer to a "normal" format (a), or to the common practice of giving these tests in public schools as summative assessments (b), or to any kind of universal norms for all testing (d).

31. A: By analyzing the results of administering norm-referenced tests to their students, educators can compare the performance of individual students with that of students in the normative samples. They *can* also compare their students' average score to the average scores in the norm samples (b). They can satisfy *both* federal (c) *and* state (d) legal accountability requirements for federal funding by showing sufficient scores, because the federal education department delegates many decisions about allocating federal funds to state education departments.

32. D: Relative to standards-based education, research shows opportunity to learn is the strongest influence on student achievement at the school level. Therefore, students are given multiple opportunities to demonstrate achievement, and repeated practice toward skill mastery rather than low grades for poor initial performance (b). At classroom levels, teachers consistently use rubrics/other scoring guides to give students criterion-referenced feedback in frequent formative assessments (d), which are more effective than only norm-referenced percentage scores in annual summative assessments (c). Regular progress reports improve teacher evaluation of learning objectives as well as student achievement more than reporting only annual standardized test results (a).

33. B: The U.S. Department of Education (ED) does fund, but does NOT develop, curriculum standards for public schools. State education departments develop them using federal (ED) funding (c). State standards are available in print and online today; online is the easiest way for teachers to access them, particularly updates to them (c), which can be published online more timely and frequently than printing these. The Common Core State Standards,

developed by a consortium of state school officers and governors with ED funding, have been adopted by most U.S. states voluntarily rather than via federal mandate (d).

34. A: Having curriculum standards and associated frameworks gives education stakeholders a common language for communicating the learning expectations they share and discussing educational processes, enabling more effective educational partnerships. Curriculum standards also provide common referents to coordinate, not individualize (b), educational system functioning across schools and districts; clarify common expectations for all students regardless of their individual demographics (c); and provide schools with motivation and focus for organizing, designing, planning, and implementing instruction (d) and assessment.

35. C: In this example of student PE learning, participating voluntarily in athletic activities and becoming accomplished in a specific sport are representative of the affective domain, i.e., developing and applying emotional attitudes toward a subject. Choices (a) and (d) are representative of the cognitive domain, i.e., developing and applying knowledge in a subject. Choice (b) is representative of the psychomotor domain, i.e., developing and applying physical skills in a subject.

36. D: In the most recent revision (Anderson and Krathwohl, 2001), Bloom's Taxonomy follows this sequence: Remember, Understand (a), Apply, Analyze (b), Evaluate, and Create (d). This hierarchy progresses from least to most difficult; hence (c) is incorrect. *(Note: The 2001 revision changed the order, from Synthesis (= Create) and then Evaluation, to Evaluate and then Create, in recognition that the process of synthesizing multiple ideas/sources inherently involves creating new wholes and relationships. It also changed the level names from nouns to verbs.)

37. C: Scaffolding is temporary support that teachers provide to students to enable them to accomplish tasks they cannot yet achieve alone, and which teachers gradually withdraw as students progress toward task/skill mastery. It ultimately moves the student role in learning from passive to active (a); requires students to increase their current knowledge (b); moves the responsibility for learning from the teacher to the student (c); and moves teachers from playing expert roles to facilitator and mentor roles (d).

38. A: In scaffolded instruction, first the teacher models performance of a new and/or difficult task and asks students to do Think-Alouds about it. The second step involves collaboration by students and teacher. The third step entails paired or small-group student work on the task, with teacher support as needed. In the fourth step, students practice the task independently.

39. B: The shared learning approach to instruction emphasizes the collective responsibility for learning of students, teachers, other educators, school staff, school administrators, parents, community members, and other stakeholders. The inquiry-guided (a) approach emphasizes student responsibility for independently investigating and learning. The learner-centered (c) approach requires students to take responsibility for learning and teachers to take responsibility for facilitating it. In the learning community (d) approach, each member of the learning community takes responsibility for participating and realizing learning goals.

40. D: When teachers establish organized routines and instructional activity sequences, explain these to students, and follow them consistently, this promotes both teacher-student communication and student cooperation, productive work, and higher-order thinking skills. When teachers establish comfortable, non-threatening classroom atmospheres, this is more effective than a sense of urgency (a). Clearly communicating clear teacher expectations is more effective than making students guess them (b). Teachers should inform students of transitions between ideas rather than not identifying them (c).

41. A: Metacognition involves thinking about and understanding one's own thought processes, which enables self-evaluation and self-regulation of one's own thinking. Students develop and use metacognition when they highlight text, draw diagrams, visualize concepts, use mnemonic devices apply learning strategies they have found most personally effective through experience, etc. Organization (b) is a cognitive strategy of arranging material with a structure that makes order and sense of it. Elaboration (c) is a cognitive strategy of producing additional explanation, details, etc., about a topic. Rehearsal (d) is a cognitive strategy of practicing information for retention.

42. B: Simulations are not done in real life, but are the most realistic of these activities. They enable activities students cannot do in real life, e.g., fighting wars, working in various jobs, marrying, having children, building and managing corporations, etc. Field trips (a) are done in real life. Experiments (c) are typically done in classrooms, labs, or other controlled environments, not real-life conditions. Role-playing (d) is similar to simulations, but less realistic as it does not try to simulate real conditions. Instead, students assume others' roles in speech and behavior, developing empathy, perspective-taking, and social interaction.

43. C: The instructional strategy of having students conduct observations helps them to develop objective thinking, pay attention to important details, and become more perceptive. Today's technology makes simulations much more vivid, interactive, and accessible to students than simulations without technology (a). Games are not only entertaining instructional strategies, but they also offer structure (b) via game rules. Experiments make abstract concepts real to students, and enable direct student ownership of learning (d).

44. D: Brainstorming (a) is more characterized by informality than formality, and more by creativity and originality than logic. Interviews (b) may be formal (structured), informal (unstructured), or a combination of both (semi-structured). Though structured interview questions have a logical sequence, interviews including affective topics may not be logical. Classroom discussions (c), while including rules (e.g., taking turns, avoiding cross-talk, disagreeing civilly, etc.), tend to be more informal, allowing students to express themselves.

45. A: Regarding brainstorming, the quantity is more important than the quality. The idea is for students to generate as many different ideas as possible, regardless of how viable, popular, etc. Thus (b) is incorrect. When students brainstorm, it is more important for them to produce original ideas than to be accurate (c). An especial strength of brainstorming as an interactive instructional strategy is that students get more ideas together than they could alone (d).

46. D: Cooperative learning groups are oriented to interdependence and value cooperation above competition, making them more compatible with many ELL/ELP students' collectivist cultures (a). The principles of cooperative learning promote *both* collective and individual responsibility (b) and accountability. When ELL/ELP students are culturally inhibited from asking certain questions of teachers, cooperative learning can make them comfortable asking these of classmates in their groups (c).

47. C: Students frequently want to know how they will use academic content in their lives before engaging in it. To meet this need, teachers should give them many different examples (a) and explain what preparation the content will give them for future opportunities. Students also often need to discover underlying principles independently (b), which teachers can enable by providing problems students must reason through, affording opportunities for mastery. Teachers can make cooperative learning effective through positive social pressure (d).

48. B: To help motivate students to learn, teachers can design assignments that offer challenges appropriate to the abilities and experiences of their students rather than giving every student the same challenge (a) regardless of background; set realistic, attainable performance goals and help students to set these (b); use test scores and grades to show student mastery rather than shortcomings (c); and give all students opportunities to attain the highest standards and grades, and avoid grading on a curve (d).

49. B: Among research-based practices whereby teachers can stimulate student motivation to learn, one is to criticize a specific performance by a student rather than criticize the student. Teacher criticism should also be constructive, i.e., focusing on what students can do better or differently rather than focusing on student errors (a). Teachers should avoid categorizing students as leaders or followers (c). They should also give students as much

choice and control as possible over their learning, evaluation, and performance rather than teachers' controlling all these completely (d).

50. A: According to a model of intrinsic student motivation to achieve in school, students first engage in activities they find interesting. If an activity is not immediately interesting to students, they then evaluate these based on two criteria (b): stimulation and control. If an activity subsequently becomes inadequate to either or both criteria, they then disengage from it (c) unless they are influenced by some extrinsic motivation (d).

51. C: When teachers use effective active listening strategies, they help students establish emotional connections with school as well as motivation (a) to learn, which requires feeling connected; show that teachers care about students and also establish and develop student-teacher relationships (b); demonstrate teacher attention to student concerns (c); help students feel understood; and provide models of effective listening (d) strategies that students can emulate.

52. A: Active listening incorporates techniques of giving the speaker both verbal and nonverbal signals; asking questions (b) as needed to clarify what the speaker says; restating what the speaker says in the listener's own words for confirmation or correction rather than repeating what the speaker said word for word (c); and interpreting the meaning of what the speaker says (d) for the speaker to confirm, correct, or clarify, and to elicit additional content from the speaker.

53. B: Active listening can include interpreting what the speaker says. When the speaker responds to listener interpretation by refining it, the speaker often gains insights into his/her own feelings, is more likely to feel heard by the listener (a), and may experience emotional catharsis (c) from expressing himself/herself and feeling heard and understood. The listener, rather than the speaker (d), develops skills for focusing on the speaker and inferring implicit meanings through active listening.

54. A: Open postures—e.g., uncrossed arms and legs, facing the speaker, etc.—communicate listener receptivity to speakers. Crossed arms and/or legs, being closed postures, do not communicate interest in speakers (b) but the reverse, as does sitting averted from the speaker(s). Listeners commonly use gestures unconsciously, but should become conscious of them, not vice versa (c), to prevent misunderstandings, because gestures carry different meanings in different cultures. Different cultures also regard eye contact differently (d): it signifies interest in some, confrontation in others; avoiding it signifies disinterest, dishonesty, or discomfort in some, but respect in others.

55. D: Facial expression is the aspect of nonverbal communication that most universally expresses the same emotions across individuals, relationships, situations, and cultures. Eye contact (a) is not because different cultures value it differently. While Americans might feel ignored by lack of eye contact, members of other cultures might regard it as a sign of respect. The social space (b) or distance from others that people find most comfortable during interactions, and the personal space (c) or distance between individuals while interacting, both vary across individuals, relationships, situations, and cultures.

56. C: When communicating with others, we use eye contact to communicate interest AND hostility (a), anger AND affection (b), and attraction; we also use it to gauge how others are responding (c) to us, and also to maintain the flow (d) of the conversation or discussion.

57. C: Nonverbal communication can reinforce verbal messages by accompanying them with appropriate eye and facial expressions, vocal tones, postures, gestures, etc.; it can also contradict them (a) by accompanying them with contrasting ones, to indicate verbal irony or sarcasm, or (unintentionally or intentionally) to betray dishonesty or mixed messages. Nonverbal communication can complement verbal communication or take its place (b), (d) in some cases, and/or repeat, add to (c), or emphasize (d) it.

58. B: This example illustrates reinforcing, i.e., strengthening verbal communication: the speaker realizes a verbal point he makes is weak, so he makes it seem stronger with a nonverbal communication technique of pounding the pulpit. (This could also be used to emphasize an already strong point.) The example does not illustrate the reverse (a), as a weak verbal point would not strengthen any physical gesture. Speech does not replace gesture (c) in this example, as both are used. The gesture does not repeat the verbal point (d), but rather aggrandizes it.

59. B: The first step users should take in evaluating online information is to consider the author's credentials. Then users should look for the publication date, most recent update, and current revision or edition. They should then look for the publisher, and if the information is published in a journal, its title. Users should then analyze the content critically (c), which includes determining the intended audience (d); whether the writer(s) use objective reasoning; coverage; writing style used; and finally, reading reviews by other users (a) evaluating the information.

60. D: Whether a journal published online is a secondary source (a) or a primary source, and whether it is too simple a source (b) or too technical (c) for user purposes, are all things to consider during a content analysis, which the user should conduct *after* an initial appraisal. Users should consider whether the journal is scholarly or popular (d) during the initial appraisal to decide whether it is reputable and whether its level of complexity is suitable for user needs.

61. C: Determining who publishes website information and whether the publisher is reputable (a), e.g., a university press; whether the site's information is current (b); and the education, credentials, experience, publications, institutional affiliation(s), and citations by others of the author (d), are all things the user should do during an initial appraisal of a website as an information source. Following this, the user should then conduct a more thorough content analysis, which includes determining whether the information given is fact, opinion, or propaganda (c). Skilled writers can disguise positions as facts.

62.C: Word-processing software programs like Microsoft Word make it simple to move text around, a distinct benefit to students learning to organize their writing. These programs also enable students to copy notes or outlines and paste them into compositions, and then easily type into them to expand them into more complete sentences and paragraphs (a). Although these programs have spell-check and grammar-check features, students cannot rely on these in place of knowing spelling/grammar (b), as they are often wrong. Microsoft Excel and similar spreadsheet programs enable students to input data without requiring extensive advance organizing and editing (d).

63. B: The best way to design a transition to be uniform between all activities is by establishing several mini-routines and connecting them via the behaviorist process of chaining. One mini-routine (a) would be insufficient; having various mini-routines (c) would prevent uniformity; and creating a big routine out of mini-routines (d) would be overkill.

64. D: Once a teacher designs a uniform transition to use between all classroom activities, s/he must not only model it for students (a) to observe and imitate, but also explicitly teach it in all steps to students (b) and also practice it consistently between all activities (c) in order for students to learn it and follow it regularly.

65. A: After getting class attention as the first step, the teacher should next announce to them which specific lesson they are momentarily going to begin as the second step. The third step is giving students detailed directions and establishing cues (e.g., "when I say 'go,' do this") in advance (d). The fourth step is to ask students whether anybody is unclear about what to do (c). The fifth step is to observe student activities and confirm they are following the directions (b).

66. C: When implementing a standard transition between classroom activities, the best way to address noncompliance is to have the noncompliant student(s) repeat the entire transitional sequence until they can follow it automatically. For smooth transitions, teachers should never interrupt the transitional activity (a) other students are successfully

following. Punishment (b) is not only inappropriate and damages self-esteem, but also is never as effective as positive reinforcement for promoting certain behaviors. Separating students (d) will not help them practice and learn the transition, and will exclude them from activities.

67. B: Researchers have found that the most effective teachers devote the first few weeks of each school year not to teaching an overview of content (a) or the first lessons in the first unit (c), and not to teaching the students social skills (d), but rather to teaching classroom routines and procedures. Having these in place and ensuring all students know and follow them enable classes to flow smoothly, decreasing interruptions and behavioral problems.

68. A: The best way to instruct students in classroom procedures and routines is to teach one or two key procedures a day over several days rather than trying to teach them all in one day (b), which is ineffective for students to remember them all. While teachers should hand out copies of procedures and routines on the first day and go over them with students, this alone (c) is insufficient; teachers must repeat and reinforce. They should explain reasons for each procedure/routine to students, model each (d), give examples and non-examples of following them, and have students model them.

69. D: The purpose of functional behavior analysis (FBA) is to determine what function any given behavior serves. All behaviors have a function/purpose. Behaviorists have summarized this premise with the generalization that all behaviors get something or get away from something. To modify a behavior, one must first know its function in order to teach a more acceptable or adaptive behavior accomplishing the same function. FBA does not teach functional behaviors (a), determine whether a behavior is functional or not (b), or make analyzing behaviors functional (c)—if conducted correctly, the analysis will be functional by defining the behavior's purpose.

70. B: Behavior contracts involve agreement by a student to do specified things for specified rewards. They teach students verbal obligations and responsibility (a), self-control and self-monitoring skills (c), and skills for negotiating and compromising (d). However, students engage in observational and vicarious learning (b) by observing the behaviors of others and the rewards they receive, and then imitating those behaviors to obtain similar rewards rather than by participating in behavior contracts.

71. C: Teachers should consider that school-age children and adolescents are NOT good at anticipating the consequences of their behaviors in advance (a) because they are oriented to the here and now. They can understand cause-and-effect relationships, but only if they are close together (b) in sequence. Any future consequences of their actions do not seem real to them (c) because their orientation to the present means they find it hard to imagine the

future. They have not yet mastered time concepts, which are still developing, and they typically have difficulty with planning skills (d).

72. B: One effective method for communicating teacher expectations to students is preparing achievement contracts defining mutual teacher-student expectations and having students sign these when school years begin. Teachers lead by example in modeling integrity for students by always behaving fairly and consistently in class, showing how they meet their own high expectations so students understand better what is expected of them; "Do as I say, not as I do" does NOT apply (a). Teachers must reinforce expectations daily for students, not periodically (c), and repeat them continually. Teachers should tell parents their expectations for both students and parents (d).

73. A: It is true that some students are motivated to work harder to please teachers when teachers get to know them and let students see them as real people. However, this does not mean teachers should become students' friends (b): they must stay in charge. It is not counterproductive, but enhances student knowledge, engagement, and ownership of expectations, to have students periodically write about how they think they are progressing and offer suggestions for improving class (c). To foster mastery learning, teachers should let students revise any work that received poor grades (d).

74. B: Research finds that when teachers learn about their students, interact and communicate with them, and give them appropriate feedback, the relationships they develop make teaching and learning more effective. The research has accumulated a significant body of literature showing the influence of teacher-student relationships on student academic achievement as well as behavior (a); hence (d) is incorrect. Teacher respect for students and guidance of students to respect each other promotes active learning; student respect for teachers does not inhibit it (c).

75. D: When students are given opportunities to interact and communicate with each other, they can hear and consider each other's ideas, and every student can have a voice, particularly in small-group discussions (a). Student-student communication promotes student sharing of the responsibility for learning (b). Another benefit of student-student interactions is that students can shape the direction of the class (c), as well as being exposed to and discussing diverse viewpoints (d).

76. C: Many research studies have found that when teacher enthusiasm is combined with constructive feedback, students are able to learn with enhanced quantity and quality; hence (a) and (b) are incorrect. Research studies also find that teachers who are more enthusiastic devote more time both to their instructional presentation and to positive feedback (d) about student performance.

77. C: Effective teachers use nonverbal behaviors not only to express excitement, but also to reinforce verbal expressions (c) of encouragement, etc. They express excitement by opening their eyes widely, raising eyebrows, etc.; express interest and connection with eye contact; and listen to students (a) with their eyes as well as their ears. Gestures like hand movements, body swinging, and sweeping arm motions communicate enthusiasm, pleasure, displeasure, amusement, disappointment, disapproval, and other emotions (b). Effective teachers move around the classroom not only to monitor students, but also to maintain student interest by being less predictable (d).

78. B: Initiative is the foundation that enables the other four components of innovation curriculum by initiating them and supporting individualized, decentralized learning activities. Inquiry (a) involves student curiosity, questioning, exploration, and research toward innovation. Invention (c) involves applying learning to real life and improving problem-solving skills on a regular, not occasional, basis. Imagination (d) involves generating divergent alternatives and creative expression.

79. A: Writing across the curriculum is an instructional practice that stimulates student Imagination by combining arts, sciences, and other subjects, and extending universal instructional themes across content areas. Having students instead of teachers ask most of the questions (b) promotes student Inquiry. Giving students more practice (c) applying what they learn promotes student Implementation. Developing student self-efficacy (d) through teachers' challenges, encouragement, and support promotes student Invention.

80. C: Text-to-speech software, like speech-to-text software, other software programs, adaptive keyboards and other adaptive hardware, and computers themselves, are considered high-tech AAC devices/systems, which are more complex and expensive. Dry-erase boards (a), like folders, binders, albums, and other easy-to-use, inexpensive image transmission and storage mechanisms, are considered low-tech. Overhead projectors (b), like tape recorders, are considered mid-tech. Simple Voice Output Communication Aids (VOCAs) are considered mid-tech, but more complex VOCAs are considered high-tech (d).

81. C: Based on their greater teaching experience and expertise, mentors can help teachers by giving them ideas and strategies to address student content knowledge gaps (a); informing them about specialized subject vocabulary (b); helping them with decisions related to relative emphases on various content areas (c); and offering them resources for accessing information (d).

82. D: Mentors can help teachers plan instructional units so they align with performance standards (a); offer teachers strategies for developing higher cognitive skills and skills for

lifelong learning (b); help teachers with writing lesson plans and also with connecting lessons coherently (c) within units; and help teachers plan varied challenges, activities, and other experiences that require and enable students to extend and apply information they have acquired from their texts and teachers (d).

83. A: Mentors can help newer teachers to understand appropriate amounts of material to include in each lesson; equal student needs for clear directions and regular reviews (b); the importance of activating and building upon prior student knowledge, including connecting it with new learning, as well as of applying new learning (c); and understanding that task difficulty levels should be increased gradually and sequentially (d).

84. B: Research shows increasingly that teacher collaboration raises new teacher retention rates (a), correlates positively with student achievement (b), and promotes higher personal satisfaction in teachers (c). Yet despite these positive effects, mentoring and other forms of teacher collaboration are utilized in the minority of schools, even in states with funding (d) for mentoring programs.

85. D: Experts recommend that to foster collaboration among teachers, school leaders should earmark resources for supporting classroom observation, planning, and mentoring; cultivate senses of shared responsibility in all faculty members (a); and recruit experienced teachers, both for the induction and mentoring of new teachers (b) and also for teacher professional development (c).

86. A: Case studies by researchers find that teachers collaborate by meeting to review student work, see if it addresses state/district standards, and improve instruction accordingly (b); forming teams to self-plan their own professional development and to align lessons across grade levels (c); receiving regular support from lead teachers or coaches; and accessing data to inform instructional decisions and planning, as well as sharing their planning time (d).

87. D: Secretary Duncan has said in multiple speeches that the near future of public education will be shaped by attracting the most talented individuals to the teaching profession rather than the largest numbers (a), and also retaining the most talented teachers (b), which he believes will require not just minimal (c) but "massive" cultural changes, but will be worth it by attaining "extraordinary" long-term impacts (d).

88. C: The TEACH.org project to improve future teacher preparation and hence student education was started by the U.S. Department of Education or ED (a) and then reformed as a public-private partnership with the Microsoft Corporation (b). Another ED initiative, Project

RESPECT (Recognizing Educational Success, Professional Excellence and Collaborative Teaching), is related to the TEACH.org project (d) and recruits teacher input about teaching reform, federal budget proposals, education in the global economy, etc.

89. A: By gathering information through meetings, interviews, and surveys, schools can identify family and community strengths and needs as bases for developing policies and programs to involve and partner with them. Broad-based community involvement and effective partnerships are found to improve learning for all students (b) by showing them connections between school curriculum and real-world skills (c). School, family, and community partnerships are found to benefit all partners (d).

90. B: By conducting community needs assessments, school action teams can develop not only approaches for community outreach (a), but also goals for involvement programs that they can further develop into full policies (b) for community involvement. They would not develop full-blown school policies for community involvement immediately (c), but develop involvement programs with goals first. They should not stop at these goals, but continue developing them into full involvement policies (d).

91. A: PDCs offer trainings that every teacher can take which help them align their PD goals with those of their school districts. Goals that teachers, their mentors, and the PDCs set must meet the standards of their state education departments (b). In addition to offering trainings, PDCs also work directly with individual new teachers (c) and their mentors to help them set PD goals that meet district guidelines. The same SMART requirements for writing objectives also apply to PD goals (d)—Specificity, Measurability, Attainability, Relevance/Results-orientation, and Time-limitation.

92. B: The ISTE helps educators both develop technology-based professional development (PD) programs and also integrate technology into instruction (b) rather than only the latter (c). The ISTE also has established standards for educational technology application, and instructs educators not only about these standards, but also about how to use peer coaching and classrooms to teach them to others (d).

93. A: ISTE teaches in-depth PD knowledge and its own educational technology standards to educators. This includes instruction in what conditions are essential for implementing these standards in classrooms (b), throughout schools at the building level (c), and across entire school districts (d). For comprehensive educational technology integration, one would expect such training to include the classroom, school, and district levels.

94. C: The trainings named are designed for and offered to school principals and administrators, not to all public school personnel (a), not to teachers and similar educators (b), and not to both faculty and administrative workers (d). These trainings target the roles, responsibilities, backgrounds, and perspectives of administrators relative to technology integration in teaching, learning, and educator professional development.

95. D: Although there is truth to the saying, "Hindsight is 20/20," this does not mean reflecting is pointless (a): it reinforces the fact that while we view our behaviors subjectively or not at all in the moment, reviewing them later affords more objectivity (b). Teachers who reflect regularly on their classroom work can identify behaviors and areas needing improvement, and plan and implement improvements accordingly—to both their interactions with students and their instructional practices (c)—based on their analysis of these (d).

96. D: To use reflection for self-assessing classroom effectiveness and planning, and implementing improvement measures accordingly, teachers should record baseline levels as early in the school year as possible rather than wait (a). They can make video recordings for objective documentation when feasible, but regular journaling (b) is more practicable, and indispensable for developing reflective skills. To show, often accurately, the learning opportunities they offer all students, teachers should select one high-achieving and one low-achieving student and track how their professional relationships with each develop (c). Writing honestly and rereading their entries regularly help teachers change their own behaviors (d).

97. C: Peer assessment and the "critical friend" method (a), wherein colleagues give teachers observational feedback on their instruction, help teachers by noticing things the teacher does that s/he cannot see and offering different perspectives. Systematic incident analysis (b) helps teachers gain insights into student behaviors and their interactions with students. Collecting and reviewing portfolios (d) helps teachers review their longitudinal work development and changes. Pre-designed self-assessment checklists, questionnaires, and other tools (c) are best for helping teachers systematically evaluate their own instructional practices, weaknesses, and strengths.

98. A: Research finds that summarizing content from texts, discussions, lectures, notes, etc., helps to improve student reading comprehension while contrasting (b), i.e., identifying differences; comparing (c), i.e., identifying similarities; and classifying (d), i.e., grouping things by similarity and organizing groups by difference or level. All of these help to improve student comprehension of complex concepts.

99. A: Cognitive research studies have determined that learning to summarize material and take notes effectively develops students' higher-order cognitive skills for analyzing